When Women and Mountains Meet

ADVENTURES IN THE WHITE MOUNTAINS

When Women and Mountains Meet

ADVENTURES IN THE WHITE MOUNTAINS

by

Julie Boardman

The Durand Press
Etna, New Hampshire

Copyright 2001 by Julie Boardman. All rights reserved. The author published an article, "Lucy Crawford," in the June 1996 issue of *Appalachia*. Portions of the chapter about Lucy Crawford have been adapted from that article.

ISBN   0-9708324-1-9

Imprint is last number shown: 9 8 7 6 5 4 3 2 1

Typesetting by May10 Design, West Lebanon, New Hampshire. The text is set in Adobe Garamond and Berthold Garamond. Printed in the United States of America.

Cover illustration: Winslow Homer (1836-1910), *In the Mountains*, 1877. Oil on canvas, 61.0 x 96.5 (24 x 38 in). Courtesy of the Brooklyn Museum of Art, the Dick S. Ramsay Fund. Winslow Homer visited the White Mountains in 1868 and 1869. It is not known whether this painting is from sketches that Homer made in the White Mountains or from the Adirondacks and Catskills where he spent time after his visits to New Hampshire.

Table of Contents

v

Preface

THIS BOOK TELLS the story of the women who helped shape the rich history of New Hampshire's White Mountains. I was inspired to write it when I began looking into the life of Lucy Crawford, the author of a famous history of the region. As I learned something about Lucy's accomplishments, I realized that she had never received the attention that she deserves, and I wondered if other women might have suffered a similar fate.

My initial research involved reading all of the White Mountain histories and scouring every issue of *Appalachia*, the journal of the Appalachian Mountain Club (AMC), from 1876 to the present day. This took some time, but it resulted in a list of several dozen women. As I investigated further, I discovered that many of these women had contributed significantly to the region. However, with the passing years, as so often happens with women, especially those who lived in the nineteenth century, their names have been forgotten.

Once I knew that I had enough material for a book, one of my first decisions centered on which women to include. Most the women whom I have chosen to write about had a special feeling for mountains. They loved being in the mountains, were curious about them, and looked to them for adventure, inspiration, or solace. Some were hikers and mountaineers, while others enriched the region as writers, artists, scientists, conservationists, explorers, innkeepers, or simply as characters.

The first women of the White Mountains were the Native Americans, but I have included little information about them. Not much is known about the Native Americans of the region, and the names that are remembered are largely male. The two exceptions are Weetamoo and Molly Ockett, and I have briefly told their stories.

Also, I have not written much about contemporary women, primarily because I had difficulty evaluating the importance of their achievements. Guy and Laura Waterman encountered the same problem when they wrote *Forest and Crag*. In the introduction to that book, the Watermans stated, "When it comes to events after about 1950, we grow skeptical of the ability of historians to form objective judgments. Until more time has elapsed to put recent events into perspective, we're all guessing as to what's important, what's really happening out there."

The first eight chapters of *When Women and Mountains Meet* follow a chronological format. My goal has been to trace the history of the White Mountains as a tourist destination and to show how people experienced the mountains in different eras. The ninth chapter describes a much-loved White Mountain character, and the tenth profiles women who performed remarkable feats on Mount Washington and the Presidential Range. The last chapter focuses on conservation efforts in the late twentieth century. Finally, an Appendix presents brief biographies of some women who were not included in the earlier chapters yet they deserved mention.

The women of the White Mountains were a fascinating group. I have enjoyed getting to know them, and I hope the readers of this book will too.

A Chronology of Women in the White Mountains

c. 1773   Deborah Vickers is the first woman to come through the White Mountain Notch (Crawford Notch).

c. 1778   Nancy, a servant to Colonel Joseph Whipple, dies of exposure in the White Mountain Notch.

c. 1805   Margaret (or Jessie) Guernsey discovers the Flume in Franconia Notch.

1817   Lucy Crawford comes to the White Mountain Notch to care for her grandfather. In November, she marries her cousin, Ethan Allen Crawford.

1821   Eliza, Abigail and Harriet Austin become the first women to climb Mount Washington.

1825   Lucy Crawford and a woman from Boston climb Mount Washington.

1831   Hayes Copp marries Dolly Emery and brings her to his homestead in Pinkham Notch.

c. 1840   Mrs. Daniel Patch is the first woman to climb Mount Moosilauke.

1846   Lucy Crawford publishes her *History of the White Mountains*, the first chronicle of the region.

1851   The Atlantic and St. Lawrence Railroad extends its tracks from Portland, Maine, to Gorham, New Hampshire.

1852   Mary Rosebrook becomes the hostess of the first Summit House on Mount Washington. She is the first woman to spend the night on the mountain.

1855   Lizzie Bourne dies on Mount Washington. She is the first woman and the second person to succumb to the mountain's notorious weather.

1861-65 The United States Civil War

1872-77 Lucia Pychowska, Marian Pychowska, and Edith Cook explore the Mahoosuc Range, and probably make the first female ascents of Bald Cap, Mount Ingalls, Mount Carlo, and Goose Eye Mountain.

1874   Eluthera Freeman and Placentia Durgin (daughters of Lucy and Ethan Allen Crawford) become the first women to climb Mount Washington in the winter.

1876   The Appalachian Mountain Club (AMC) is founded. At the club's second meeting, women are admitted to membership.

1878   Edith Cook and the Pychowskas meet Isabella Stone and start writing letters about their mountain explorations.

1881   After celebrating their fiftieth wedding anniversary, Hayes and Dolly Copp leave their farm and part ways.

1882   The Cooks and Pychowskas spend the summer at the Ravine House in Randolph, New Hampshire, and begin building paths in the northern peaks of the Presidential Range.

1882   Martha F. Whitman, Dr. Laura Porter, and Charlotte Ricker explore the Twin Range with Augustus E. Scott of the AMC. They are the first women to climb North Twin Mountain, South Twin Mountain, Mount Bond, and Bondcliff.

1883   A party that includes Edith Cook and Suzie M. Barstow makes the first exploration of the entire Carter-Moriah Range.

1884   Marian Pychowska and Suzie M. Barstow discover the Pinnacle in Huntington Ravine.

1884   Isabella Stone and George Russell explore Mount Waternomee, determining its location and structure.

c. 1885   Martha Knowles, an active AMC member, makes a complete traverse of the Presidential Range in one day. This is probably the first Presidential traverse by a woman.

1889   *Fishin' Jimmy* by Annie Trumbull Slosson is published.

1891   Katherine Sleeper opens Wonalancet Farm.

1897   Annie Smith Peck completes a Presidential traverse.

1898   Under Katherine Sleeper's leadership, the Wonalancet Out Door Club is founded.

1899   Mr. and Mrs. F.O. Stanley drive their steam-powered automobile to the summit of Mount Washington.

1901   Ellen McRoberts Mason and eight men found the Society for the Protection of New Hampshire Forests.

1911   The Weeks Act is signed into law, providing the basis for the creation of the White Mountain National Forest.

1914-18 World War I

1914   Katharine Sleeper Walden leads an effort to have the Bowl, a tract of land between Mount Whiteface and Mount Passaconaway, included in the White Mountain National Forest.

1916   Frank Mason introduces his family, including his daughter Margaret Helburn, to rock climbing. This marks the beginning of the rock climbing movement in New England.

1923   Willard and Margaret Helburn organize an active winter climbing group known as the Bemis Crew.

1926   Miriam O'Brien, encouraged by her climbs in the White Mountains, goes to Europe to become a rock climber. Over the next few years, she will "dazzle the mountaineering world with her exploits."

1930   The Fishin' Jimmy Trail is named after the character from Annie Trumbull Slosson's most popular story.

1932   Florence Murray Clark makes a solo ascent of Mount Washington by dog sled.

1941-45 World War II

1957   Miriam O'Brien Underhill is the first woman to climb all of the White Mountain 4,000-footers.

1960   Robert and Miriam Underhill become the first people to climb the White Mountain 4,000 footers in the calendar winter.

1980   Laura Waterman, Natalie Davis and Debbie O'Neill complete a winter Presidential traverse. They are the first women to achieve this difficult feat.

1991   After years of work by Katharine Fowler-Billings and Anna Stearns, the Green Hills Preserve is dedicated.

When Women and Mountains Meet

ADVENTURES IN THE WHITE MOUNTAINS

Great things are done when women and mountains meet....
adapted from William Blake

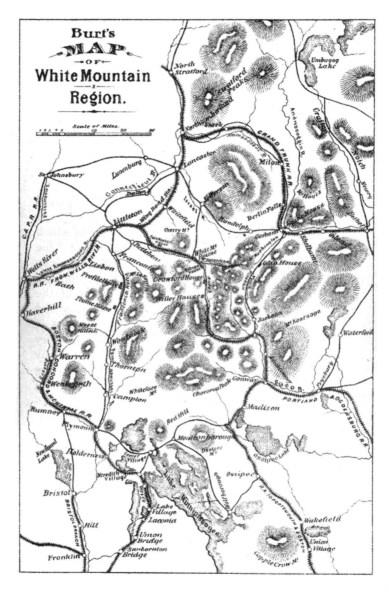

Burt's Map of the White Mountain Region from Henry M. Burt's *Guide to the White Mountains and River Saguenay*, Springfield, Mass. 1874.

1: The First Settlers

THE WHITE MOUNTAINS of New Hampshire are rugged peaks ranging in elevation from three thousand to six thousand feet above sea level. They are not particularly high as mountains go, but that does not diminish their beauty. In fact, the region features an extraordinary variety of magnificent scenery: dramatic snow-capped mountains, gentle hills, romantic valleys, terrifying cliffs, wild and lovely cascades, hidden pools with emerald-green water, and much more.

It took centuries for people to discover these charms. For a long time, no white men or women went to the White Mountains with the exception of a few adventurers like Darby Field, who climbed Mount Washington, the highest peak in the Northeast, way back in 1642. After 1763 and the end of the French and Indian War, the region was finally safe for habitation, and the first settlers came. They established their homesteads in the fertile lands that bordered the rivers—in settlements such as Lancaster, New Hampshire, along the Connecticut River, and Conway, New Hampshire, along the Saco. Although the pioneers lived among the mountains, they were too busy struggling to survive to take much interest in them. If anything, they saw the mountains as hostile places, as something to be overcome.

Around 1771, Timothy Nash, a resident of Lancaster, New Hampshire, found a gap in the mountains that could be used as a passage from the settlements in the upper Connecticut River valley to the seacoast. A few years later, a rough trail was cut through this gap, which had come to be known as the White Mountain Notch. Today it is known as Crawford Notch.

Soon after the path was made, two hardy women came up through the White Mountain Notch on their way to Jefferson, a settlement that was known as Dartmouth until 1796. Both women—Nancy Barton and Deborah Vickers—have earned a lasting place in White Mountain history.

A third woman from this era—Molly Ockett—also became famous. She is one of the few Native American women whose name has come down to the present day.

No one knows how these three women felt about mountains, for they did not leave any record of their lives. However, their stories have been told from generation to generation, and, clearly, they were remarkable women who met the challenges of a mountainous region with confidence and courage.

NANCY BARTON

One of the most famous and tragic White Mountain stories involves a servant girl named Nancy Barton, who worked for Colonel Joseph Whipple, one of the largest landowners in Jefferson. The Nancy story has many variations. The version presented here is based on what Lucy Crawford wrote in her *History of the White Mountains*. F. Allen Burt, author of *The Story of Mount Washington*, felt Lucy's account was "the most reliable source for the facts of this tragedy."

Nancy and a young male servant in Whipple's household fell in love, and the couple decided to go to Portsmouth to be married. Nancy, who had carefully saved her earnings, entrusted her money with her fiancé and went to Lancaster to buy some items for the journey. On her return, she was distressed to learn that her prospective husband had taken her money and left for Portsmouth with Colonel Whipple.

Although it was early December, and snow was deep upon the ground, Nancy set out after them, ignoring family members who pleaded with her not to make a trip alone through an uninhabited region. Nancy was determined to go for she felt sure the pair would be spending the night at a special camp in the Notch. Upon her arrival, she found only the embers from their fire. Con-

Nancy in the Snow *from* The Heart of the White Mountains *by Samuel Drake.*

fident that she could overtake the men, Nancy continued on her journey. After trudging for several more miles, she crossed a stream and soaked the bottom of her dress. By this time, she was probably hungry and exhausted from her long trek, and she lay down by a tree to rest. She never got up again. The next day, a search party from Colonel Whipple's household found Nancy's frozen body by the side of the stream. According to Lucy Crawford, when Nancy's lover heard of her fate, he went mad and died a few months later. These tragic events took place around 1778.

The stream that Nancy crossed is known today as Nancy Brook. She is also commemorated in Nancy Pond, Nancy Cascades, Mount Nancy, and the Nancy Pond Trail.

GRANNY STALBIRD (DEBORAH VICKERS)

Deborah Vickers, one of the first female settlers in Jefferson, New Hampshire, came there to work in Colonel Joseph Whipple's household. After Vickers had been with Whipple a year, he tried to pay her for her service in valueless continental currency. When Vickers realized what the Colonel had done, she protested vigorously and Whipple placated her by giving her fifty acres of land. Soon thereafter, Vickers married Richard Stalbird and they settled on the land and remained there for the rest of their lives.

Some Native Americans had taught Deborah Stalbird about the healing properties of roots and herbs, and after her husband died, she made use of this knowledge as she traveled around the countryside restoring people to health. She became a beloved figure, known throughout the White Mountains as Granny Stalbird.

Lucy Crawford's *History of the White Mountains* describes an incident involving Granny Stalbird, whom Lucy refers to as Granny Starbard. In 1821, Ethan Allen Crawford cut his heel with his axe while clearing a path from his home to the foot of Mount Washington. His fellow workers helped him back to his farm where he found Mrs. Stalbird, now an elderly woman whose "head was whitened with more than eighty years." Although Ethan's wound was bandaged and had stopped bleeding, Stalbird wanted to examine it. Ignoring Ethan's complaints, she unwrapped the bandages, and the wound began to bleed again. Using Ethan's words, Lucy described what Stalbird did next: "She…went into the field, plucked some young clover leaves, pounded them in a mortar, and placed them on my wound; this stopped the blood so suddenly that it caused me to faint…."

Another story about Granny Stalbird pays tribute to her steadfast nature. One dark night, while on her way to see a patient in Shelburne, she encountered a heavy rainstorm and found refuge under a huge boulder resting on a ledge. As lightning flashed and thunder broke around her, she patiently held her horse by the bridle, remaining there until the next morning. After that, the ledge came to be known as Stalbird's Ledge. Later, it was blasted to bits by the workers who constructed the railroad line to Gorham. Fortunately, Granny Stalbird found a more lasting memorial in Stalbird Brook, which is found in Jefferson.

MOLLY OCKETT

Molly Ockett (also known as Molly Lockett, Molly Ackett, Mollyocket, Mollocket, Mollyrocket, Moll Ockett and Mollymocket) was a Native American woman born sometime in the first half of the eighteenth century, perhaps around 1730. Like Granny Stalbird, Molly Ockett had expert knowledge of the medicinal use of herbs, roots and bark. She traveled up and down the valley of the Androscoggin River, ministering to the settlers. Although her travels took her primarily through western Maine, she occasionally visited the White Mountains of New Hampshire.

Several stories recall Molly Ockett's involvement with the people of the towns she visited. Each spring she carried seed corn to a Conway resident, Colonel McMillan. On one occasion, she left her sack of corn by an old log, and someone named Lydia Fisher picked it up and had it ground into meal at Noah Eastman's mill, giving rise to the following poem:

> Molly Ockett lost her pocket,
> Lydia Fisher found it,
> Lydia carried it to the mill,
> And Uncle Noah ground it.

Another story credits Molly Ockett with saving the life of a Colonel Clark of Boston who visited the White Mountains yearly to trade for furs. A cruel Indian named Tomhegan intended to kill Clark, but Molly Ockett learned of his plan. She traveled many miles through the wilderness to reach Clark's camp in order to warn him. She arrived just in time, and Clark fled to safety. According to some accounts, Clark wanted to reward Molly Ockett for her loyalty, and when she was old and infirm, he brought her to live with his family in Boston. However, civilized life did not suit Molly Ockett and she left, explaining that she wanted to be "in the great forest, amid the trees, the companions of her youth."

In her final years, Molly Ockett lived in Andover, Maine. She was converted to Catholicism and was christened Mary Agatha. She died in Andover in 1816 and was thought to be close to ninety years of age. A headstone with the following inscription marks her grave: "MOLLOCKET Baptized Mary Agatha, died in the Christian Faith, August 2, A.D., 1816. The Last of the Pequakets."

Molly Ockett's name has been given to several geographic features. All are found in areas she covered in her travels: Mollidgewock Brook, which is near Errol, New Hampshire; Mollywocket Brook, which flows into the Androscoggin River near Berlin, New Hampshire; and Molly Lockett's Cave, which is located on the trail to Jockey Cap, a ledge near Fryeburg, Maine. Molly Ockett used the cave as a shelter.

The people of Bethel, Maine, still honor this eighteenth century Native American woman in an annual Molly Ockett Day.

2: The Beginning of White Mountain Tourism

C LIMBING MOUNTAINS was a relatively new pastime in the first part of the nineteenth century. For centuries, people had avoided mountains, viewing them as wild and terrifying places. As these attitudes about mountains gradually changed, the idea of climbing them for pleasure began to take hold. Recreational mountain climbing started in Europe in the last quarter of the eighteenth century, but the climbing impulse took longer to develop in the United States. However, around 1820, as the young nation began to prosper, the first tourists with an interest in ascending Mount Washington arrived in the White Mountains. A remarkable family was there to assist them.

LUCY CRAWFORD

Lucy Crawford was an early settler in the White Mountain Notch and helped develop it as a tourist destination. She was one of the first women to climb Mount Washington—an achievement that might not seem particularly noteworthy, but in 1825, when she completed her climb, it took true courage and determination. And she was the author of *History of the White Mountains*, the first chronicle of the region. If Lucy had not written this engaging book, a lot of information about the beginning of White Mountain tourism might have been lost forever.

Despite these contributions, Lucy Crawford is a forgotten figure today. Her husband Ethan Allen Crawford and her father-in-law Abel Crawford are still remembered, primarily because Lucy's book celebrates their lives. Every White Mountain historian after Lucy Crawford has discussed the Crawford men. The hardships these early innkeepers endured, their adventures as White Mountain guides, Ethan's hunting exploits and his legendary strength—all of this is described in detail. It is obvious these writers drew their information from Lucy's book, yet they gave her little credit and said virtually nothing about her part in developing the Notch as a vacation area.

Tourism was unknown in the White Mountains when Lucy Crawford was born in 1793. The mountains were unexplored and generally regarded as unfriendly places. By 1869, the year she died, the White Mountains would be one of America's most famous vacation areas. Several railroads would serve the region, and many thousands of people would visit each summer.

Lucy Crawford was born Lucy Howe in Guildhall, Vermont, a small settlement along the banks of the Connecticut River, not far from Lancaster, New Hampshire. A close-knit community, Guildhall abounded with people named Howe, Rosebrook, and Crawford, some of whom had intermarried. The relationships among the families are hard to untangle, but it is only important to understand this link: Eleazar and Hannah Rosebrook were among Guildhall's early settlers, and their eldest daughter Mercy married Samuel Howe of Guildhall. Samuel and Mercy Howe were

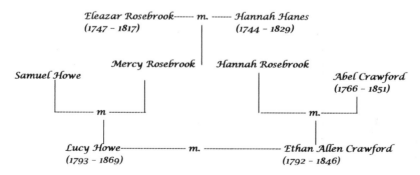

The Crawford-Rosebrook family relationship. As this chart shows, Ethan Allen Crawford and Lucy Howe Crawford were first cousins. (Their mothers were sisters.)

Lucy's parents. The Rosebrook's second daughter Hannah married another young man from Guildhall, Abel Crawford. Hannah and Abel Crawford were Ethan Allen Crawford's parents.

A year or so before Lucy's birth, her uncle, Abel Crawford, moved across the river to New Hampshire and took up residence in a small log hut located a few miles above the White Mountain Notch. The Notch was a narrow, rugged passage dividing two great ranges of the White Mountains. The sheer rock walls of what is now Mount Webster, at the southern end of the Presidential Range, rose on one side of the Notch, and the peak now known as Mount Willey of the Field-Willey Range rose on the other. A rough trail had been blazed through this mountain gap, and people were beginning to use it to transport goods between the settlements in the upper Connecticut River valley and two thriving seacoast towns, Portland, Maine, and Portsmouth, New Hampshire. This provided a shorter route than going up around the north side of the mountains, and Abel Crawford probably sensed that opportunities were there for an enterprising young man eager to serve travelers.

Not long after Abel Crawford settled in the White Mountains, Eleazar Rosebrook, Abel's father-in-law as well as Lucy's grandfather, decided to take part in the development of the new trade route. He purchased Abel's property and Abel moved his family down to Hart's Location, twelve miles away.

In 1803, after the state legislature granted funds for a turnpike through the Notch, Rosebrook built a large two-story house that looked out on Mount Washington and other peaks of what would eventually be known as the Presidential Range. Rosebrook and his wife began operating an inn to provide food, drink and a place of rest for the travelers who came through the Notch in everincreasing numbers. Abel Crawford and his wife did the same at the other end of the Notch.

Meanwhile, Lucy Howe was growing up in Guildhall. Little information is available about Lucy's early years, but a small item in

Lucy Crawford, around 1860.

the *History of Lancaster, New Hampshire* indicates she was a spirited, athletic girl. The history describes two "horse blocks" that stood in front of the old Lancaster meetinghouse. Most women used them to mount their horses, but "a few of the more sprightly girls would disdain the horse block and mount from the ground by placing their hands on the necks of the horses and springing into the saddle." Lucy Howe of Guildhall is mentioned as one of these girls.

Lucy may have attended a village school, or she may have been taught at home, for her mother had been given a good basic education. Whatever the means of instruction, Lucy learned to read and write well enough that Stearns Morse, the Dartmouth College professor who edited a twentieth century edition of her history, claimed she could have held her own with present day college freshmen.

In the spring of 1817, Ethan Allen Crawford (Abel's son and Lucy's cousin) made a special trip to Guildhall to ask Lucy if she would go to the White Mountains to help take care of their grandfather. Eleazar Rosebrook had a serious cancer of the lip, and with his children grown and scattered, he needed someone to act as a nurse. Since Lucy was an unmarried woman in her twenties with no family responsibilities, she was a natural choice. In addition, she had always been a "particular favorite" of her grandparents. Lucy agreed to go, probably thinking that her visit would be a brief one. A few months earlier, Ethan Allen Crawford had answered a similar call for help. Rosebrook promised to give Ethan the deed to all his property if he would assume Rosebrook's debts and manage the farm and tavern.

Eleazar Rosebrook died in September of 1817, and about six weeks later, in early November, Lucy Howe and Ethan Allen Crawford were married. From Lucy's explanation, it sounds as if the wedding of the two cousins was based on practicality rather than any romantic attraction. She wrote that Rosebrook came up with the idea of the marriage, thinking it might be convenient if Ethan had Lucy around to help look after their grandmother and a feebleminded son who still lived at home. Lucy added that Ethan admired her "judgment, alacrity, and perseverance" in caring for their grandfather and had no one else to fill her place. For those reasons he asked her to become his wife.

Lucy had just turned twenty-four at the time of her wedding. A picture taken when she was in her sixties suggests she may have been rather plain as a young woman, but she worked hard and seldom complained—excellent qualities for a pioneer wife. Just shy of twenty-five, Ethan was over six feet tall and renowned for his strength. (In her history Lucy referred to him as "the mountain giant.") He also had a reputation as a great talker, a rural raconteur with a rich fund of anecdotes about hunting bears and other incidents of mountain life.

Almost from the beginning of the marriage, their lives were star-crossed. The following July, Lucy gave birth to their first child, and that very day a fire raged through their house. Although everyone escaped without injury, the fire destroyed their home and Ethan and Lucy lost almost all of their belongings. With help from some neighbors, Ethan moved a small house (it probably had been part of Rosebrook's property) to the site of their old home and set to work making it comfortable for the winter. The Crawfords recovered from the terrible fire, but it would be just the first in a series of disasters that would plague them during their years in the White Mountains.

As Ethan added to and improved the house, the inn prospered. In winter, when snow covered the ground, hundreds of horse-drawn sleighs loaded down with pork, cheese, butter, and other goods passed through the Notch each week. Many of the drivers stopped to spend the night at the inn, sometimes filling the house so far beyond its capacity that Lucy had to make up a large bed on the floor for the guests to use.

We know about the settlement of the Notch and the Crawford's trials during their early years there because Lucy wrote about it in her history. She also described how Abel and Ethan Crawford expanded their inn business by promoting the mountains as a place of outdoor adventure. During the summer of 1818 and the spring of 1819, three parties of men came to the Crawford inns to climb Mount Washington. No path ran through the forest, and thick undergrowth made the ascent difficult, so difficult that one party of climbers came back to Lucy and Ethan's house with their clothes badly torn. This interest in climbing gave Abel and Ethan Crawford the idea of clearing a path to Mount Washington's summit. In 1819, they cut a rough trail from a spot near the present Crawford Hostel up through the woods to the top of Mount Clinton (also known as Mount Pierce). The path continued above tree line, crossed the southern peaks of the range, passed two small ponds (the Lakes of the Clouds), and ascended to the summit of Mount Washington. Known today as the Crawford Path, it is the oldest continuously used hiking trail in the United States.

After blazing their trail, the Crawfords advertised it in newspapers, and visitors began coming to their inns strictly to climb Mount Washington. Among the first to arrive were some men from nearby Lancaster who, in 1820, hired Ethan to guide them up the new trail so they could give names to the high peaks of the range. Mount Washington had received its name around 1784, but none of the other peaks had yet been named. After reaching Mount Washington's summit, the men drank toasts with a plentiful supply of "O-be-joyful" as they named four mountains after the four presidents who served after George Washington—Adams, Jefferson, Madison and Monroe. They also named a peak after Benjamin Franklin and called another Mount Pleasant. Today this peak is known as Mount Eisenhower.

The view from Lucy and Ethan Allen Crawford's Old Moosehorn Tavern. The White Mountains, from the Giant's Grave, near the Mount Washington House. *Plate #1 by Isaac Sprague, for William Oakes'* Scenery of the White Mountains.

By 1830, the Crawford family was running three separate inns to accommodate all the visitors to the Notch. Tom Crawford (Ethan Allen Crawford's brother) ran the Notch House, located near the trailhead for the Crawford Path. The Gate of the Notch of the White Mountains, with the Notch House. *Plate #5, by Isaac Sprague, for William Oakes'* Scenery of the White Mountains.

The trailhead for the Crawford Path was several miles from Ethan and Lucy's inn, and guests had to travel over a rough, hilly road to get there. As the number of visitors who wanted to climb Mount Washington increased, Ethan asked Charles Stewart, a young lawyer and surveyor from Lancaster, to help him find a new way up the mountain. In the spring of 1821, Ethan and Stewart entered the woods with a compass and blazed a route that originated at Ethan and Lucy's inn and followed the Ammonoosuc River over level ground for nearly seven miles to the foot of the mountain. From there, climbers could ascend a big ridge that extended to the summit. That summer, Ethan hired some men to help him clear this second path. The present road from Route 302 to the Base Station of the Cog Railway follows much the same course as the path Ethan Crawford and his helpers carved out of the wilderness.

As word spread about the beauty of the White Mountains and the adventure of climbing Mount Washington, more and more tourists came to the Notch. By 1830, the Crawford families were operating three separate inns to accommodate all of the visitors. Tom Crawford, Ethan's brother, and his wife were proprietors of the Notch House, which opened in 1829 near the place where the Crawford Path originated. About eight miles to the south, Abel and Hannah Crawford ran the Mount Crawford House, and about four miles to the north, Ethan and Lucy Crawford had their inn, which was known as the Old Moosehorn Tavern.

Ethan and Lucy worked hard to make their guests' stay comfortable and pleasurable. Ethan purchased a cannon and placed it outside the inn. When he fired the cannon, the great booming noise bounced from hill to hill. Everyone enjoyed the echo, which some people called "Crawford's home-made thunder." Ethan also

Abel and Hannah Crawford ran the Mt. Crawford House, located at the southern end of the Notch. The Mt. Crawford House in 1875. Photograph by Fred E. Crawford.

produced a clear, bright echo with a long tin horn. In addition, he entertained guests with tales about the mountains and his experiences while hunting and trapping. "His fund of bear stories was almost inexhaustible," wrote Benjamin Willey, the author of an early history of the White Mountains.

While Ethan charmed the guests, Lucy occupied herself with innkeeping and family responsibilities. Between 1818 and 1835, she gave birth to ten children—five girls and five boys. The second child died in infancy; the other nine were healthy children who grew to adulthood. Lucy felt her children benefited from being part of an innkeeping family, because the visitors offered them "good counsels, by which they gradually acquired good morals and business habits..."

Indeed, much could be learned from the guests, for Lucy and Ethan's Old Moosehorn Tavern attracted a clientele that included some of the most famous men and women of the day. In her book, Lucy recorded the visits of Daniel Webster; Alden Partridge, one time Superintendent of the United States Military Academy at West Point and founder of the military academy at Norwich, Vermont; and James Kent, Chief Justice of the New York Supreme Court. Other well-known visitors not mentioned in Lucy's history were Nathaniel Hawthorne, Ralph Waldo Emerson, Washington Irving, Charles Sumner, and the noted British author Harriet Martineau.

Some of the guests wrote about their visits. Nathaniel Hawthorne described an evening he spent at Lucy and Ethan's tavern in a sketch published in the *New England Magazine* in 1835. He pictured Ethan as "a sturdy mountaineer, of six feet two and corresponding bulk, with a heavy set of features, such as might be moulded on his own blacksmith's anvil, but yet indicative of mother wit and rough humor." Other writers depicted Ethan (usually in vivid terms), but no one left a portrait of Lucy. In fact, of all the travelers who wrote about visiting the Crawford inns, only Harriet Martineau mentions the women, and her comments give just a glimpse of their behind-the-scenes role:

The Crawfords, who live twelve miles apart, lead a remarkable life, but one which seems to agree well with mind and body. They are hale, lively men, of uncommon simplicity of manners, dearly loving company, but able to make themselves happy in solitude. Their year is passed in alternations of throngs of guests with entire loneliness. During the long dreary season of thaw no one comes in sight; or, if a chance visitor should approach, it is in a somewhat questionable shape, being no other than a hungry bear, the last of his clan. During two months, August and September... a flock of summer tourists take wing through the region. Then the Crawfords lay down beds in every corner of their dwellings, and spread their longest tables, and bustle from morning till night, the hosts acting as guides to every accessible point in the neighbourhood, and the women of the family cooking and waiting from sunrise till midnight. After the 1st of October comes a pause, dead silence again for three months, till the snow is frozen hard, and trains of loaded sleighs appear in the passes.

The inn business flourished, yet a series of problems still bedeviled Lucy and Ethan. In 1826, a heavy rainstorm destroyed some of their property and much of the Notch road. This same storm caused a landslide that killed the Willey family who lived just a few miles away. Two years later, another storm inflicted further damage. To better serve guests, Ethan improved his property and eventually built a new house, and this meant that he had to take out loans and mortgage the farm. Trouble in another form came from a devious neighbor who schemed to steal inn business from them. And then to make matters worse, throughout the 1830s, Ethan's health steadily deteriorated.

In 1836, Ethan was jailed in Lancaster for failure to pay his debts, and he remained there for twenty-five days, even though he was desperately ill. When he was released, his friends and family persuaded him to give up the inn and farm. Lucy and Ethan turned their property over to the mortgage holders—Thomas Abbott, Nathaniel Abbott, and Zara Cutler—and in 1837, they returned to their native village, Guildhall, Vermont.

Although Lucy knew she had no choice in the matter, she was leaving the Notch with reluctance, and she expressed her remorse at the foreclosure. During her early years in the Notch, someone had suggested that Lucy keep a diary. She began making notes of what went on at the inn, for she knew that there was "something very extraordinary" about their lives. People must have known about this diary, for at the foreclosure one of the mortgage holders suggested that Lucy use it to write a history of their years in the White Mountains. She could publish the book, and it might bring in enough money to get their home back. Lucy was encouraged when the Abbotts and Zara Cutler promised to return the property to the Crawfords if they could come up with the funds to repay the loan with its interest.

While she was living in Guildhall, Lucy began working on her history of the White Mountains. Since she was retired from the hotel business, she had only her family to care for, and this gave her some extra hours for writing. When her chores were done, Lucy would take out her pen and paper, and, using her diary and the guest registers from the inn, she would carefully put down her memories of the years that she and Ethan had spent in the White Mountain Notch.

By the time Lucy completed her manuscript, the Crawfords were back in the Notch. They returned there in 1843 and rented a house within sight of their old home. Both Lucy and Ethan still felt the sting of losing their homestead. They desperately wanted it back, but soon after their return, the mortgage holders made some false promises and duped Lucy and Ethan into signing a paper that took their home from them for good.

Lucy was furious when she realized what had happened. The Lucy Crawford Papers at Dartmouth College contain the draft of a letter Lucy wrote to Zara Cutler. Although undated, the letter was obviously written soon after she had learned about the mortgage holders' deceit. "I intend to get facts and put them on paper and sometime they will be published," she warned. Perhaps to appease her, Thomas Abbott assisted Lucy in getting her history published. Having recently moved to Portland, Maine, he spoke on Lucy's behalf with F.A. & A.F. Gerrish, printers in that city. The correspondence also suggests that Abbott may have advanced some money to pay for the printing.

Lucy Crawford's history was first issued in 1846 under the title *History of the White Mountains, From the First Settlement of Upper Coos and Pequaket.* Nine hundred and sixty copies were printed, and Lucy agreed to undertake the sale of the book herself.

It is a fascinating book. Lucy described the courage and hardships of the early residents of Coos County and recounted year by year the significant events of the life that she and Ethan had led in the White Mountains. She drew liberally from the inn's guest albums, sometimes quoting complete entries. The book is more a narrative of the Crawford family's perils than a history. Yet a picture of the lives of the early settlers emerges, and interspersed in the narrative are some of the famous stories of the White Mountains: the story of Nancy, for example; and the legend of the Great Carbuncle that inspired a Nathaniel Hawthorne short story after he heard it told at the Crawford tavern.

The book is written as though Ethan is telling the story. In the introduction, Lucy explains that she tried to use "his own language, as nearly as she could." Because the book uses this narrative device, some people have given Ethan Crawford credit as the history's author. However, Lucy states unequivocally that the work was her own, and considering Ethan's declining health, which affected his mind, it is hard to imagine how he could have had much of a hand in the writing. In fact, by the time the book was published, Ethan Allen Crawford had died. He contracted typhoid fever in the fall of 1845, continued in poor health throughout the following winter and passed away in June of 1846 at age fifty-three. The extensive revisions that Lucy made to the history in the 1850s provide further evidence of her authorship.

After Ethan's death, Lucy and the children went back to

Guildhall, but within a few years, two of the older Crawford daughters moved to Lowell, Massachusetts, to run a boarding house for mill workers. Eventually the entire family moved to a factory village where they could all "live together in useful employment." As the years passed and her children married and established their own homes, Lucy lived with one child after another, always going wherever she could be most helpful.

It is unlikely that Lucy earned much money from the sale of her book. However, for years, she clung to the hope that she might somehow regain her old homestead, and the idea of raising money by selling her book persisted. Sometime in the 1850s, she began revising the book. She included more travel information about the mountains and used the third person instead of Ethan's words to tell the story of their lives. She added material about Ethan's final years and told a tangled story about the deceit of the mortgage holders. Deciding that illustrations would enhance the book, she hired an artist named Marshall Tidd to do some drawings depicting local scenes and the feats of "the mountain giant."

The Crawford family cemetery near Fabyans, just off Route 302.

Lucy applied for a copyright in 1860, but then, for unknown reasons, she gave up her efforts to bring forth a revised book. Perhaps the printing costs were simply too much for her to pay. Luck always seemed to run against the Crawfords, and Lucy would not live long enough to see another edition of her history published. She died in 1869 and was buried next to Ethan in a family burying ground near the road leading from Route 302 to the base of Mount Washington.

Lucy's original history was reissued (with some supplementary descriptive material about the White Mountains) in 1883 and again in 1886. In the middle of the twentieth century, pieces of her revised history began to emerge from the attics of Crawford descendants where they had languished since her death. Stearns Morse of Dartmouth College took the original history and added material from the revised manuscript to create a book published by the Trustees of Dartmouth College in 1966. Twelve years later, the AMC issued a new edition of Morse's edited work that included Marshall Tidd's drawings. They had been found and donated to Dartmouth by William Crawford Wheeler, a great, great grandson of Lucy and Ethan Crawford.

Lucy Crawford's *History of the White Mountains* is still in print. A vividly written account of the early pioneers in Crawford Notch and the beginning of tourism, it is one of the great classics of White Mountain literature.

ELIZA, HARRIET, AND ABIGAIL AUSTIN
The First Women To Climb Mount Washington

On August 31, 1821, shortly after Ethan Allen Crawford had completed his second path to the summit of Mount Washington, three young women—Eliza, Harriet, and Abigail Austin—from nearby Jefferson, New Hampshire, came to the Crawford inn and told Ethan they wanted to climb the mountain. Eliza Austin was engaged to marry Charles Stewart, the man who had helped Ethan locate the new path, and no doubt, Stewart had talked to her about the new route to the summit. No women had ever made the ascent, and, according to Lucy's history, the sisters "were ambitious and wanted to have the honor of being the first females who placed their feet on this high and now celebrated place, Mount Washington."

What the sisters planned to do was not easy. The AMC *White Mountain Guide* has this to say about the climb:

> Inexperienced hikers sometimes misjudge the difficulty of climbing Mt. Washington by placing too much emphasis on the relatively short distance from the trailheads to the summit. To a person used to walking around the neighborhood, the trail distance of 4 mi. or so sounds rather tame. But the most important factor in the difficulty of the trip is the altitude gain of 4000 ft., give or take a few hundred, from base to summit. . . . To a person unused to mountain trails, and in less than excellent physical condition, this unrelenting uphill grind can be grueling and intensely discouraging. If you are not an experienced climber or a trained athlete, you will almost certainly enjoy the ascent of Mt. Washington a great deal more if you build up to it with easier climbs in areas with less exposure to potentially severe weather.

The Austin sisters were not experienced climbers or trained athletes, and unlike today's hikers who can drive to the trailhead, they had to walk seven miles just to get to the base of the mountain. In addition, they wore long dresses as they walked over a newly cut trail, which was full of roots and rocks, and then up the steep, rocky slopes to the summit of Mount Washington.

Since none of the sisters left any description of their adventure, we have to rely on what Lucy Crawford recorded. We learn that the women were accompanied by three men: their brother, a tenant on their Jefferson farm who carried the baggage, and Charles Stewart. The first day the party walked as far as a camp that Ethan had built along the path. Dividing the camp into two chambers, one for the women and one for the men, they spent the night. The next day they climbed to another camp, which they again divided into two rooms. Unfavorable weather forced them to remain there for two nights.

By this time, they were running out of food. Many people would have been discouraged by these hardships, but the Austin sisters were women of iron resolution. The tenant farmer, who was anxious to get back to his chores, went back to the Crawford's inn and asked Ethan to take his place. Bringing fresh provisions, Ethan joined the group, and the next day he guided everyone to the summit where they had a splendid view of the surrounding countryside. Lucy wrote that the Austin sisters were "richly paid for their trouble." She added, "I think this act of heroism ought to confer an honor on them, as everything was done with so much prudence and modesty by them; there was not left a trace or even a chance for a reproach or slander excepting by those who thought themselves outdone by these young ladies."

After the sisters' successful ascent, Lucy Crawford was particularly eager to climb Mount Washington. However, Ethan strongly

To help women ascend Mt. Washington more easily, Ethan Allen Crawford built two facing camps—one for men and one for women. They were destroyed by a heavy rainstorm in 1826. The Two Camps Before the Slide. *Woodblock drawn by Marshall M. Tidd.*

believed mountain climbing was an activity for men, not women, and he would not allow her to try. Fortunately, an opportunity finally arose in August of 1825 when a man from Boston and his sister arrived at the inn. The sister was determined to climb the mountain, even though many people tried to discourage her. She asked Lucy to come along, and Ethan finally consented.

Lucy, Ethan, the gentleman and his sister walked a total of eighteen miles and camped out for two nights because of rainy, foggy weather. When they finally reached Mount Washington's summit, the rain had cleansed the air and the views were breathtaking. Lucy described the experience in glowing terms:

> We could look in every direction and view the works of nature as they lay spread before us—could see towns and villages in the distance, and so clear was the atmosphere that we could distinguish one house from another; but should I attempt to describe the scenery, my pen would fail, for want of language to express my ideas of the grandeur of the place.

Although Ethan still had doubts about women's ability to climb Mount Washington, he began doing what he could to make the climb easier for them. He built two facing camps, one for men and one for women, and he improved his second path so that ladies could ride to the base of the mountain and save their strength for the climb. By the late 1820s, many women were climbing to the summit of the mountain, and like the Austin sisters, they were "richly paid for their trouble."

Eliza, Harriet, and Abigail Austin were probably the first women in the United States to climb a significant mountain. Through their persistence and determination, they provided an inspiring example for the many women climbers who have followed them.

3: The Railroad Reaches the Mountains

I N 1851, the Atlantic and St. Lawrence Railroad extended its tracks from Portland, Maine to Gorham, New Hampshire, becoming the first of several railroads that would eventually reach the mountain region. Prior to that time, people had to use two or more means of transportation—train, stagecoach, and sometimes a steamboat—to get to their destination in the mountains, and the journey took several days. After the railroad was completed to Gorham, someone could board the train in Boston in the morning and, with a change of trains in Portland, be in the heart of the White Mountains by late afternoon.

The railroad profoundly affected tourism in the White Mountains. Almost immediately, Gorham became a major tourist center with large first-class hotels. One such hotel was the White Mountain Station House, which served both as railroad depot and hotel. Eight miles away in the Glen, a scenic area at the base of Mount Washington, construction began on the Glen House. Opened to the public in 1853, the Glen House was the first of the grand resort hotels, which became such an important feature of the White Mountains in the second half of the nineteenth century.

Before 1851, most tourists climbed Mount Washington from the west, using the original Crawford Path or Ethan Allen Crawford's second path. After the railroad reached Gorham, people began ascending the mountain from the east, using the Glen House Bridle Path. The completion of the Carriage Road (today's Auto Road) in 1861 did even more to expand the tourist trade on the eastern side of Mount Washington.

The Glen House was the first of the grand hotels in the White Mountains.

Two women who ran inns in this part of the mountains became well known during this period, and their names live on in
White Mountain geography. A third woman has faded into ob-
scurity, but she deserves to be remembered for her unusual role as
the first woman innkeeper on the summit of Mount Washington.

DOLLY COPP

Lucy Crawford was probably typical of the early women innkeepers in the White Mountains. She remained in the background,
cooking and cleaning and looking after her numerous children,
while her husband charmed the guests. Lucy's name might have
been forgotten completely if she had not written her famous history. However, over on the other side of the Presidential Range,
another woman innkeeper named Dolly Copp thoroughly enjoyed
meeting the public. People knew and talked about Dolly during
her lifetime, and today a popular campground bears her name.

Dolly Copp, whose maiden name was Dolly Emery, grew up
in Bartlett, a little village along the Saco River not far from

Crawford Notch. In 1831, Dolly married Hayes Copp and moved to his homestead on the eastern side of Mount Washington in Martin's Location, north of Pinkham Notch. When a road was built between Jackson and Randolph, it ran right by the Copp's farm, and, like many other families living on well-traveled thoroughfares, Hayes and Dolly began taking in overnight guests. Hayes Copp was a silent, sullen man—not the sort to entertain people with stories or take the extra time to make their visit comfortable. Dolly, on the other hand, was spirited and outgoing. She was the one visitors remembered, and they usually referred to the inn as Dolly Copp's place, almost as if Hayes were not there.

As a young woman, Dolly had a slim figure, blond hair, a fair complexion, and tiny feet of which she was particularly proud. Although she made all her own clothing, she always bought fine shoes in Portland so she could show off her feet. Added to this picture of femininity, Dolly smoked a short-stemmed clay pipe.

Dolly was a master of all the household arts. As her biographer George Cross wrote, "No other housewife wove so many bolts of woolen homespun, so many yards of linen, could match her dyes of delicate blue, could rival her golden butter, rich cheese

The Copp homestead in Pinkham Notch. Photograph by Guy Shorey.

Dolly Copp in her later years.

and maple syrup." The Copp homestead was just down the road from the Glen House, and soon after the hotel opened, J. M. Thompson, the owner, began sending guests down to the Copp farm so they could admire and purchase Dolly's remarkable handicrafts and the products of her kitchen. Dolly took delight in being able to profit from the booming business at this nearby hotel.

The Copp farm's other tourist attraction was its view of a cliff that looked like a misshapen human profile. Dolly is credited with naming the profile "the Imp." Many people associated her so closely with the profile that they sometimes referred to it as "Dolly Copp's Imp."

In *The Heart of the White Mountains*, Samuel Drake described a visit he made to the Copp farm around 1880 or 1881. On arriving at the house, he found "all the members of the household and all the inmates of the barn-yard" there to greet him. The years had transformed Dolly. She was in her late seventies by this time and no longer petite. Drake wrote that she "stood in the door-way, which her ample figure quite filled, trifling with the beads of a gold necklace." He described Hayes Copp as an "an old man, whose countenance had hardened into a vacant smile...."

Dolly Copp has become famous in White Mountain history because of what supposedly happened when she and Hayes celebrated their golden wedding anniversary in 1881. According to the story, Dolly waited until the party had ended and then declared, "Hayes is well enough. But fifty years is long enough for a woman to live with any man." With that, she left her husband and went off to live with her daughter in Auburn, Maine. Hayes Copp spent his remaining years being cared for by a relative in his old hometown of Stow, Maine. Dolly's independence captured people's imagination, and she is remembered today in the Dolly Copp Campground, which is located on the site of the old Copp homestead.

SARAH HAYES

A few miles away in Gorham, another woman innkeeper achieved cartographical immortality for nothing more than her pleasing personality. Mount Hayes, a small mountain at the western end of the Mahoosuc Range, was not named in honor of the American president Rutherford B. Hayes, as some might think. Instead, it honors Sarah Hayes, a woman from Bangor, Maine, who, in the early 1850s, managed the White Mountain Station House (later known as the Alpine House) in Gorham. Some people claim that Thomas Starr King, the author of *The White Hills: Their Legends, Landscapes and Poetry*, gave Mrs. Hayes' name to the mountain. In his book King wrote, "Mount Hayes takes its name from the excellent woman whom visitors in Gorham, some three years since, have occasion to remember with gratitude as a hostess of the hotel. It is now her monument." King thought highly of Mount Hayes and claimed its summit was the perfect spot for viewing Mount Washington.

By 1853, there were two hotels on the summit of Mount Washington: the Summit House (built in 1852) is on the right, and the Tip-Top House (1853) is on the left. From Historical Relics of the White Mountains *by John H. Spaulding.*

MARY ROSEBROOK

In 1852, three enterprising men—Nathan R. Perkins of Jefferson, and Lucius M. Rosebrook (a son of pioneer innkeeper Eleazar Rosebrook) and Joseph S. Hall, both of Lancaster—built a small stone building on the summit of Mount Washington. Known as the Summit House, it opened in late July and provided meals and accommodations for people who wanted to dine or spend a night on top of the highest mountain in the Northeast.

Mary Rosebrook, Lucius Rosebrook's wife, became the first hostess of the Summit House. Many years later, the Rosebrook's daughter, Mary Rosebrook Ackert, sent a letter to *Among the Clouds*, a newspaper published on the summit of Mount Washington in the summer months. She began her letter as follows:

> I often see mention made of the men who first opened the way to make Mt. Washington what it is at the present day, but I think with them, that the brave pioneer women ought to share their glory. When father, with Mr. Hall,

had about completed the Old Summit House in 1852, they were planning how they should entertain and accommodate their guests without the aid of a woman. Mother told them she would go. They said she would not dare, but she insisted that she would.... She stayed all night at the Glen House, and I have often heard her say that as she looked from her window at the almost inaccessible heights, that her heart almost failed her. She mounted a four-year-old colt, that had never been up the mountain before, and prepared to make the ascent. A gentleman who was stopping at the Glen House came and gave her two dollars, for her courage, he said, in making the attempt. She made the ascent safely, and was the first woman to stay all night on Mount Washington.

Mary Ackert went on to describe her mother's contribution as the "genial landlady of the Old Summit House." She explained that Mary Rosebrook cooked, served meals, and performed many special services for her guests. To give an example, Ackert told about a party that arrived at the Summit House wearing insufficient clothing. One of the women was so numb with cold she could barely speak. As Ackert wrote:

> Mother put her to bed in warm blankets and gave her warm drinks and soon she was all right. In the morning mother cut up blankets and made them underclothes and mittens, so that they could make the downward journey without the danger which attended their ascent.

From the very first, the Summit House did a brisk business. It opened in late July of 1852, and when it closed six weeks later, the receipts totaled over two thousand dollars. This success inspired several men to build a competing hotel, the famous Tip-Top House, which opened the following summer. Having two rival hotels on the summit was not practical, and in 1854, both hotels came under the same management. Lucius Rosebrook sold his share in the Summit House at that time. Mary Rosebrook retired from her duties as a mountaintop innkeeper, and the Rosebrooks left the mountains for a new home in the Midwest.

4: Mount Washington's Most Famous Victim

MANY TOURISTS wanted to spend the night at one of the summit houses on Mount Washington in the 1850s. Most people were not aware of the strong winds and sudden storms that are characteristic of the mountain's weather, and no one thought much about the possible danger of climbing to the summit—until a tragic death occurred, one that is famous in White Mountain history.

LIZZIE BOURNE

Over the past century and a half, more than 120 people have died on Mount Washington and the Presidential Range. One of the most celebrated casualties is the first—Frederick Strickland. The son of a member of the British Parliament and an heir to a large estate, Strickland died in October of 1849 while foolishly hiking alone in snowy, windy conditions. Two other memorable victims are William Curtis and Allan Ormsbee, distinguished amateur athletes who perished in a savage storm on the last day of June in 1900 while hiking up the Crawford Path to attend an AMC field meeting at the Summit House. Their deaths spurred the AMC to build a small refuge hut near the place where Curtis died and ultimately to construct the Lakes of the Clouds Hut.

Although these three fatalities are well known, they are not the most famous victims of Mount Washington. That dubious honor belongs to Lizzie Bourne, a twenty-three-year-old woman from Kennebunk, Maine. On September 13, 1855, Lizzie left the Glen House in Pinkham Notch with her uncle, Kennebunk shipbuilder George Bourne, and his daughter Lucy, planning to climb Mount

This is the only known photograph of Lizzie Bourne.

Washington and spend the night at one of the summit houses. Shortly after coming to the end of the partially completed Carriage Road, they encountered bad weather, yet they continued their ascent. The weather grew worse, and the party was benighted not far from the summit, which was hidden from their view by a cloud. During the night, Lizzie Bourne died. Lizzie was young and pretty and very near shelter, all of which added to the poignancy of her death. The place where she passed away was marked with a pile of stones and eventually a wooden monument. It became a tourist attraction almost immediately, and it is still one today.

Although the Lizzie Bourne tragedy has been written about extensively in books, magazines, and newspapers, the descriptions of the event differ significantly. September 14 is frequently given as the date of her death, and other dates (September 15, September 24) appear in some versions. Many writers have embellished the story with picturesque but questionable details: Lizzie waves a handkerchief to friends as she sets off from the Glen House. She insists on continuing the climb even though some workmen on the Carriage Road urge the party to turn back. She sings gaily as she and her uncle and cousin huddle together behind some rocks near the summit. Or alternatively, she loses her bonnet, staggers and falls down, dying immediately. As for the cause of Lizzie's death, some writers attribute it to exposure or hypothermia, while others claim she suffered from heart disease.

Perhaps the best source of information about what happened is a letter written by George Bourne shortly after Lizzie died. Several newspapers had stated incorrectly that the Bourne party had lost its way on the mountain, and many people had criticized George Bourne for not hiring a guide. In response to all of the false reports about the tragedy and his part in it, Bourne wrote a letter to *The Boston Journal* presenting what he termed "a correct account of the whole affair." Bourne's narrative begins as follows:

> On the evening of Wednesday, the 12th inst., our little party, consisting of Henry A. Jones, esq., and lady of Portland, Elizabeth, daughter of Edward E. Bourne, my wife, daughter Lucy and myself, arrived at the Glen House, intending in the morning to ascend Mount Washington.

Bourne explained that it rained early Thursday morning, so they postponed their trip. The weather cleared by ten, however, and immediately after lunch, Lizzie persuaded her uncle and cousin to start for the summit. Having been told the path was easy to follow, George Bourne "saw no necessity of a guide and consequently took none." When they set out it was two o'clock in the afternoon. The weather was fine, and the girls were "elated at the prospect of realizing the fulfillment of their long anticipated desire—that of spending a night on Mount Washington."

The Bournes began walking up the Carriage Road, which was under construction at the time. For the first two and one-half miles, Dillon P. Myers, one of the contractors for the road, walked with them. After Myers parted ways with the Bournes, they continued their climb "in high glee, occasionally stopping to admire the scenery...." At four o'clock, they came to the end of the road and "made inquiry" (probably of some workers) and were told the summit was two and a half miles away and the path was obvious.

George Bourne's letter says nothing about warnings not to continue, nor does he mention that Lizzie urged them to go on. Today, few people would attempt to climb the remaining two and a half miles to the summit at such a late hour. However, in the mid-nineteenth century, tourists did not appreciate the danger of Mount Washington's sudden weather changes, and they frequently started for the summit in the afternoon.

As the Bournes resumed their hike, they followed the Glen House Bridle Path. It was quite steep and the footing was poor. Upon reaching the top of what George Bourne referred to as a "large knowle or mountain, called the Ledge," they encountered a violent wind. The wind soon lulled, however, and the young women were eager to keep going. When they reached the top of another steep pitch, they discovered another high hill stood before them. They kept climbing one pitch after another, always expecting they would soon be at the summit. During their climb, the fierce wind presented the greatest difficulty, according to George Bourne.

As the Bournes went up what they thought was the last pitch, the sun was setting, and they paused briefly to enjoy the beauty of the scene. Bourne wrote, "It was in ascending this steep that Elizabeth began to show signs of weariness, and needed assistance, but the assurance that this was our last ascent, gave us encouragement to persevere." They trudged wearily onward, but when they reached the top of the slope, they found they had still further to go.

Although they did not know it, they were very close to the summit. In good weather, they certainly would have seen the summit houses and realized that they were near shelter, but instead, a cloud obscured the view. The Bournes could dimly see the path, so they continued to climb. However, Lizzie had to rest frequently, and they made little progress. Finally, darkness closed in and they could no longer make out where they were going. At this point, George Bourne considered what to do:

> It was very cold, and the wind blowing a gale, the night dark and fearful, and we upon a bleak mountain without a shrub, rock, or tree, under which to find shelter. What

was to be done? To lie down and commit our souls to the keeping of a merciful Father, probably to sleep that death that knows no waking? This was my first thought, for I was well nigh worn out with fatigue myself. But a few moments' reflection dissipated these impressions, and I resolved to do what I could for our preservation. So violent was the wind that it was impossible to adjust the ladies' shawls to any advantage, but we did the best we could, and they laid themselves down in the middle of the path, as we had not lost our way, while I went to work to build a wall of such loose rocks as in the darkness of the night I could lay hands upon, to protect them from the blast.

Bourne managed to erect "quite a breastwork." Lucy and Lizzie seemed comfortable, and he felt sure he could keep them safe until morning. Bourne lay down next to the young women to keep them warm. Whenever he felt cold, he got up and warmed himself by looking for more rocks, always returning quickly to the girls. According to his letter, he never left them for more than ten minutes.

About ten o'clock, he lay down at Lizzie's back and taking her hand found it to be "icy cold." Her forehead was also cold, and she failed to respond when he spoke to her. "She was dead—had

Lizzie's body was carried to the Tip-Top House where attempts were made to revive her.

uttered no complaint, expressed no regret or fear, but passed silently away."

George Bourne spent the rest of that "long, long, weary night" trying to keep himself and his daughter as warm as possible. When dawn finally came, they were amazed to see how near they were to the summit. They set out for the Tip-Top House, where they aroused the inhabitants and told their sorrowful story. Two men and two women went to retrieve Lizzie's body and bring it to the house. They attempted to revive her "with hot rocks and hot baths," but they could not "call back her spirit" and finally abandoned their efforts. Meanwhile, a messenger-boy had gone down to the Glen House to inform George Bourne's wife of the tragedy. Around ten in the morning, Joseph Hall, a White Mountain guide and co-owner of the summit houses, came up to help. He and three other men carried Lizzie's body down to the Glen House in a shallow wooden box.

Bourne concluded his account by writing, "Suffice it to say, that no one suggested our need of a guide, neither did we find one necessary, as we did not miss our way. Still, as the event proved it would have been well for us to have taken a guide."

Bourne's letter makes it clear that Lizzie Bourne died on September 13. He stated that his party arrived at the Glen House on September 12, and their ascent of the mountain and Lizzie's demise took place the following day. Newspapers also confirm September 13 as the correct date. Both *The Boston Post* and *The Boston Journal* ran a short paragraph about the tragedy. Both dispatches bore a September 14 dateline and reported that the death had occurred the day before.

At the time of the tragedy, most people felt Lizzie Bourne died from exposure to the cold weather, and George Bourne's description of his niece's condition on the climb suggests she was in the early stages of hypothermia before they were benighted. However, in a postscript to his letter, George Bourne offered another explanation: "From all circumstances, it is now evident that Elizabeth did not die from the cold alone, but from some organic affection of the heart or lungs, induced by fatigue and exposure."

The idea that Lizzie Bourne died of heart disease is also mentioned in a letter written by Lizzie's father, Edward E. Bourne. A leading citizen of Kennebunk, Bourne served as the judge of probate for York County, Maine. On September 20, 1855, he wrote a letter to Joseph Hall, who had carried his daughter's body down the mountain. After thanking Hall for his help, Bourne supported his brother's decision to climb the mountain without a guide and stated, "The principal cause of the fatality was not in the wind, or the cold, but in some internal defect, of which she had frequently spoken to her friends."

During the first days after Lizzie Bourne died, her family members probably went over the events of the tragedy repeatedly and speculated about the cause of her death. They may have been comforted by the idea that she suffered from heart disease, and this undoubtedly would have taken some pressure off of George Bourne. Although Lizzie might have had a heart condition or "some internal defect," no medical evidence exists to confirm this conclusion about the cause of her death.

The Lizzie Bourne Monument on Mt. Washington. This photo shows how close to the summit Lizzie Bourne was when she died.

After Lizzie Bourne died, people who climbed the mountain began adding stones to the pile of rocks that George Bourne had built up as protection and which marked the spot where Lizzie had died. Before long, they had created a sizeable cairn. When the Cog Railway was built in 1869, it passed right by the cairn. The railway managers must have recognized the value of the site as a tourist attraction, for they erected a board monument on the cairn that gave her name, age and date of death. Although, over the years, the monument has been replaced and the inscription has been changed, the site of Lizzie Bourne's death is still commemorated on Mount Washington.

Edward Bourne, Lizzie's father, had hoped to place a formal memorial to his daughter on the spot where she died, and he hired a stonecutter to produce a large four-sided obelisk. However, the company constructing the Carriage Road failed in 1856, and all work on the road stopped for several years, making it impossible to transport the memorial up the mountain. It was placed instead at Lizzie's gravesite in Hope Cemetery, Kennebunk, Maine.

The monument has the following inscription on the front:

> Lizzie C. Bourne
> Aged 23 years
> Daughter of Edw. E. Bourne
> of Kennebunk, Maine
>
> Here in the twilight cold
>   and gray,
> Lifeless, but beautiful,
>   she lay,
> And from the sky serene
>   and far
> A voice fell, like a falling
>   star,
> Excelsior!
>
> This monument was meant for
> the top of Mount Washington, but
> its erection there was prevented
> by the failure of the projected road.

*The Lizzie Bourne Monument in Hope Cemetery,
Kennebunk, Maine. The monument, which Lizzie's
father had hoped to erect on Mount Washington, was
placed in Hope Cemetery when the construction of the
Carriage Road was halted because of lack of funds.*

The lines of poetry are from the last stanza of Henry
Wadsworth Longfellow's "Excelsior." One change is made: the
pronoun "he" in the poem becomes "she" on the monument. The
poem is about a young man who dies on a mountain. He carries a
banner bearing the motto "Excelsior," meaning "higher." People
warn the young man not to make his climb, but he disregards all
warnings and temptations as he pursues his goal, his higher pur-
pose. Edward Bourne must have been consoled by the idea that
his daughter possessed a similar extraordinary determination. In
the letter to Joseph Hall, Bourne wrote, "Lizzie's resolution tran-
scended her physical power. No obstacle could discourage her in
her pursuit of any object which she had resolved to attain."

On the right side of the monument, the circumstances of Lizzie
Bourne's death are described:

In the afternoon of Sept. 14, 1855, Miss Bourne, with her uncle and cousin, attempted to climb this mountain, but her strength suddenly failed, from the wet cold blast. They sought the poor shelter of these rocks and here, about 10 at night, she expired in consequence it is thought of a heart disease fatally aggravated by toil and fatigue.

It seems odd that the monument gives the wrong date for Lizzie Bourne's death. However, Edward Bourne was devastated by the loss of his child. Both his wife and another daughter had passed away a few years earlier, and then Lizzie, his only remaining daughter, was taken from him. Perhaps his grief so clouded his memory he gave the stonecutter incorrect information.

The two Lizzie Bourne monuments are not the only reminders of the tragedy that took place on Mount Washington. When he went to the White Mountains, George Bourne was in the midst of decorating the exterior of his Kennebunk home with elaborate Gothic trim. On his return to Kennebunk, he began working furiously to complete the work on the house, probably in an attempt to keep his mind occupied, for he was tormented by Lizzie's death. By the summer of 1856, the job was finished. George Bourne had created a house that was so bedecked with buttresses, arches, and spires it looked like a frosted confection. Today, George Bourne's former home is known as the Wedding Cake House, and it is one of Kennebunk's most popular tourist attractions.

Sadly, George Bourne never had a chance to enjoy his remodeled home. Thirteen months after Lizzie had died, he contracted typhoid fever, and a few months later, on December 7, 1856, he passed away. Some people thought George Bourne's distress over the events on Mount Washington had something to do with his death. As Edward Bourne wrote in *The Bourne Family of Kennebunk*, "…the suffering of that night, both mental and bodily, without doubt, very seriously impaired George's physical constitution; so that it became more accessible to the attacks and ravages of disease." If this was true, then Mount Washington claimed two victims on that awful night of September 13, 1855.

5: A Poet and a Story Writer

I
F THE PERIOD when the Crawfords operated their inns was "the heroic age" of the White Mountains (a description used by Dr. Frederick Tuckerman in an *Appalachia* article), then the years from about 1850 to 1900 might be termed "the romantic age." It was a time when tourists had a passion for the picturesque and looked to the mountains as a source of inspiration.

In 1859, Thomas Starr King, a prominent Unitarian minister, published a highly successful book, *The White Hills: Their Legends, Landscapes and Poetry*, that promoted the idea of admiring mountain scenery. King claimed that he wrote his book "to direct attention to noble landscapes that lie along the routes by which the White Mountains are now approached by tourists." He believed people needed instruction to appreciate fine views, which he termed "glories of Divine art."

Mountains had to be seen from just the right place to get the most scenic value from them, according to King. For example, he decreed that the ideal spot for observing Mount Madison was the Leadmine Bridge on the Androscoggin River in Shelburne. From this location, a tourist could see the mountain towering against the sky, perfectly framed by two nearby hills. If the viewing took place in another spot, even a quarter of a mile away, the "charm of the picture" was spoiled "by breaking the frame, or cutting away the base, or shutting out some portion of the meadow foreground, or extinguishing the flashes of the silvery river."

Time of day mattered too. King said the Mount Madison viewpoint should be visited on a midsummer day "after tea, and before sunset." The best time to see the Profile in Franconia Notch was at four in the afternoon, and the optimum time for the Flume was early morning.

With all this emphasis on the ennobling qualities of beautiful views, it is not surprising that the region attracted many artists. Some women artists worked in the White Mountains in the second half of the nineteenth century, but none produced a significant body of work having the region as a subject. However, writers with an inspirational message also flourished during this period. Two such writers were Lucy Larcom, a well-known poet, and Annie Trumbull Slosson, a popular storywriter.

LUCY LARCOM

In the Ossipee Mountains, a range located immediately north of Lake Winnepesaukee, there is a gentle 2,093-foot-high hill known as Larcom Mountain. One of the few White Mountain peaks named for a woman, it honors Lucy Larcom, a nineteenth century poet and author. Larcom Mountain is adjacent to Mount Whittier, which is named for "the poet of the White Hills"— John Greenleaf Whittier. It is no accident that Larcom Mountain and Mount Whittier are close together. The two poets knew one an-

Lucy Larcom. Drawing from Lucy Larcom's Poems *(1884).*

other well, and for many years, they vacationed together at the same White Mountain inn, the Bear Camp River House in West Ossipee.

Although her name is unfamiliar today, Lucy Larcom was well known in the nineteenth century. Born in 1824, Larcom was a Lowell mill girl who contributed to the famous Lowell Offering. In her adult years, she wrote essays and poetry. Readers of that era enjoyed her poetry, which emphasized the splendor of the natural world and usually delivered an uplifting message. Many of her verses owed their inspiration to the White Mountains. *The White Hills in Poetry*, an anthology put together by Eugene Musgrove, includes twenty-four poems by Lucy Larcom. The only poet exceeding that number is Whittier with twenty-five poems.

In addition to her poetry, Lucy Larcom enriched the region by bestowing names on two mountains in the Sandwich Range. She suggested that one be called Mount Wonalancet, in honor of the son and successor of the great Pennacook chieftain Passaconaway, and that the other be called Mount Paugus, in honor of the Pennacook chieftain who died at the battle at Lovewell's Pond in Fryeburg, Maine, in 1725.

In her later years, Lucy Larcom liked to stay at the Summit House on Mount Washington. This was not the same Summit House as the one built in 1852. After the Carriage Road and Cog Railway were completed, spending a night on the summit became so fashionable that a new Summit House was needed. Opened in 1873, it accommodated one hundred and fifty guests, making it the largest hotel in America on a mountaintop. While vacationing at the new Summit House, Lucy Larcom wrote this poem:

ASLEEP ON THE SUMMIT

Upon the mountain's stormy breast
I laid me down and sank to rest;
I felt the wild thrill of the blast,
Defied and welcomed as it passed,

And made my lullaby the psalm
Of strife that wins immortal calm.

Cradled and rocked by wind and cloud,
Safe pillowed on the summit proud,
Steadied by that encircling arm
Which holds the universe from harm
I knew the Lord my soul would keep,
Among His mountain-tops asleep.

Lucy Larcom died of a heart ailment in 1893. Less than a month after her death, the AMC proposed that her name be given to a peak in the Ossipee Range. A mountain in the range had already been named for Whittier, but some confusion existed about exactly which one it was. The AMC straightened everything out, giving the name Larcom Mountain to a peak at the northwestern corner of the range and the name Mount Whittier to the peak next to it.

ANNIE TRUMBULL SLOSSON

In September of 1878, *The White Mountain Echo* listed Mrs. Annie Trumbull Slosson of Hartford, Connecticut, as a new arrival at the Profile House, a grand hotel in Franconia Notch. (Every week this Bethlehem newspaper published the names of the guests at the major White Mountain hotels.) A forty-year-old widow, Slosson was a pleasant-looking woman with dark hair, a wide mouth, and lively, intelligent eyes. This may have been Slosson's first holiday in the White Mountains, and if so, it was to be the first of many visits. For the next three decades, she would return to the mountains every year, usually coming in early June and staying for a good part of the summer. During this time she became a White Mountain personality, someone who was almost as closely associated with Franconia Notch as the famous rock formation known as the Profile.

Like Lucy Larcom, Annie Trumbull Slosson enjoyed considerable renown in the nineteenth and early twentieth century, yet

Annie Trumbull Slosson in 1913.

today her name has faded from memory. Slosson had some unusual hobbies, which she pursued avidly. She collected and was
considered an authority on fine porcelain. Entomology fascinated
her, and, even though she was an amateur, she published articles
in leading entomological journals and was well regarded by professional entomologists. However, she was best known for her stories. Slosson wrote long stories that usually taught some moral
lesson. Many were set in the White Mountains, particularly in
Franconia Notch.

A member of a distinguished Connecticut family, Annie
Trumbull was born in Stonington, Connecticut, and grew up in
Hartford. When she was in her late twenties, she married Edward
Slosson, a New York lawyer. However, just four and a half years
after their wedding, Edward Slosson died. Annie Slosson's loss was
compounded when her only sister, Mary Slosson Prime, died a
few months later.

Mary's husband was William C. Prime, a well-to-do New
Yorker who had a highly successful career as a lawyer, editor, art

connoisseur, and author. The owner and editor of the *New York Journal of Commerce*, Prime wrote books on everything from pottery and porcelain to fishing and travel. Some of the books had White Mountain settings, and Prime was highly regarded in the region's literary circles.

After their spouses died, Annie Trumbull Slosson and William Prime sought comfort in each other's company and became close friends. Annie returned to Hartford for a few years, but eventually Prime invited her to live in his New York City home. The city became their base, but Prime and Slosson spent part of the winter in Florida and most of the summer in the White Mountains. It was a highly unusual relationship by nineteenth century standards, and many people were confused about it, usually thinking Prime and Slosson were brother and sister.

Whatever the terms of their relationship (and there is no evidence they were anything but good friends), William Prime strongly influenced Annie Slosson. He probably provided the inspiration that she needed to develop her writing talent, and he served as the literary agent for some of her books. He also may have introduced her to the White Mountains.

William Prime's connection with the mountains went back many years, back to the late 1850s when he and Mary Prime first went to Franconia Notch to stay at the Profile House, one of the grandest of the grand hotels. In one of his books, Prime described the Profile House as place with "a vast drawing room" where the women wore "brilliant dresses, jewelry, and all the adornments of modern life." It was a far cry from the simple inns the Crawfords had operated in Crawford Notch a few decades earlier.

After his wife died, Prime was one of the first guests to arrive at the Profile House each summer, and often he was the last to leave in the fall. However, he did not sit on the veranda of the hotel and just gaze at the mountains like some of the guests. In addition to all his other talents, Prime excelled at fly-fishing. At first, he fished in Profile Lake, a pond located directly beneath the famous Profile (the

Old Man of the Mountain). However, as tourism increased in Franconia Notch, Profile Lake bustled with activity and the trout fishing declined. Prime and a fishing companion named William Bridge escaped from all the hubbub by climbing up to Lake Moran, a beautiful little lake on the side of Cannon Mountain that few people knew about. Prime and Bridge liked this lake so much that they bought it in 1876 and gave it a new name—Lonesome Lake. They visited Lonesome Lake frequently and entertained friends at a cabin that they built on its shore.

It is uncertain when Annie Trumbull Slosson first went to the White Mountains, but she visited every year after her friendship

The Profile House in Franconia Notch was one of the grandest of the grand hotels.

Gale Cottage was built by Annie Trumbull Slosson and William Prime in the late 1880s. Originally, a long walkway connected Gale Cottage to the Mount Lafayette House.

with Prime blossomed. Like William Prime, Slosson stayed at the Profile House. But she may have found the hotel too elegant and pretentious for her tastes, for in the mid-1880s, she and Prime transferred their allegiance to the Mount Lafayette House in Franconia, a quiet little village not far from Franconia Notch. A farmhouse-style inn that accommodated sixty people, the Mount Lafayette House was located near the Gale River, and its advertisements spoke of "first-class trout fishing within easy distance."

Soon after she began going there, Annie Slosson bought the hotel, and she and Prime built a summer cottage on the grounds. Completed around 1890, the cottage was connected to the hotel by a long covered walkway. Prime and Slosson named their summer home Gale Cottage. Surrounded by woods and offering a lovely view of the Franconia Range, Gale Cottage provided a perfect place for Annie to relax and pursue her many interests.

All her life, Annie Slosson liked to explore the natural world. At first, she focused on plants and flowers, but in early 1886, she turned her attention to entomology and, in typical fashion, embarked on her new hobby with extraordinary dedication. She collected insects in Florida during the winter and in the White Mountains during the summer. Every summer, Slosson stayed for a week or more at the Summit House on Mount Washington and spent much of her time collecting. Amazingly, Slosson found over 3,000 different insects on the bare summit cone, some of them entirely new species. Year after year, she published lists of her findings in one of the entomological journals. Some of her discoveries were given the suffix *slossonae* in her honor, and some were given the suffix *washingtonensis* in honor of the mountain.

One of the most fascinating insects on the summit is the White Mountain butterfly (*C. semidea*), which Slosson referred to as Mount Washington's oldest inhabitant. The butterfly, whose brown and gray mottled wings allow it to blend into the austere surroundings, dates from the glacial period and is only found on the Presidential Range and the very highest summits of mountains in Colorado.

So many people wanted to spend the night on Mount Washington that a new hotel was needed. This Summit House, which opened in 1873, could accommodate 150 guests. Both Lucy Larcom and Annie Trumbull Slosson stayed here.

Slosson spent so much time collecting on Mount Washington's summit that she jokingly began calling herself a tourist attraction. In an article she wrote for the *Bulletin of the Brooklyn Entomological Society*, Slosson described the reaction of summit visitors when they saw her:

> In my frequent visits to Mount Washington and my long sojourns on the summit I heard more strange and uncomplimentary comments upon myself and my doings than I ever heard at a lower level. You who have been to that delightful spot know how bleak and rugged is its external appearance and how little suggestion of animal life is there. A butterfly on that peak would seem to the casual observer or summer tourist an incongruous thing, a miracle. So each day when the train crept up the mountain, laden with travelers, looking, very often for the first time, upon the strange peak covered with pile upon pile of huge rocks, I, happily and harmlessly following my beloved pursuit below the platform, would hear such remarks as these:
>
> 'What in the world is that old woman about? What's she got in her hand?' 'Oh, it's a butterfly-net! Did you ever?' 'She must be crazy. Just think of a butterfly up here. Why do her folks let her do it?' 'Let's ask in the house about her, they'll know.' .... I tell you I know from experience how it feels to be considered 'a rare alpine aberration.'
>
> 'Come on, Ma,' I once heard a sunburned youth say to a plain, homey old woman as I stood on the platform watching the tourists filling up the waiting train soon to start for the base. 'Come, the cars is going d'rectly, we must get seats.'
>
> 'Le'mme alone, John. Seems's if I hadn't seen all the sights yet. Let's see. I've got 'em writ down here,' and she read from a crumpled scrap of paper: 'Printin' office, Lizzie Bourne's grave stun, the Tip-over House and—there I ain't seen the old bug woman!' I did not introduce myself and nobody pointed me out. So the disappointed sight-seer was dragged reluctantly to the train, her golden opportunity lost.

As this selection indicates, Slosson liked to imitate the speech of common people in her writing. She frequently did this in her stories. Her fiction-writing career began in the late 1880s with a story entitled *Fishin' Jimmy*. The main character is a simple fisherman from Franconia whose real name is James Whitcher, but he is better known as "Fishin' Jimmy." Slosson modeled the character after James Smith, a caretaker of Prime's cabin at Lonesome Lake.

One day Fishin' Jimmy wanders into a church and hears a sermon given by a minister who is vacationing at one of the hotels in Franconia Notch. The sermon is about fishing, and Fishin' Jimmy realizes that Christianity is a fishing religion (or "fishin' r'ligin" as Slosson wrote.) He is taken with the idea of answering Christ's call to become a "Fisher of Men," and from that time on, he tries to follow the Master Fisherman and live a good Christian life.

In the last chapter, the setting is the Profile House on a stormy afternoon in July. As lightning flashes across the sky and hail rattles

William Prime's cabin on Lonesome Lake. The cabin was turned into an AMC hut in 1930.

the windows of the hotel, someone remembers that two boys who are hotel guests have gone up Mount Lafayette with a dog. Then word comes that Fishin' Jimmy, who by this time is old and feeble, has started up the mountain after them. Suddenly the boys run into the hotel, reporting that the dog is lost and that they have not seen Fishin' Jimmy. A search party is formed, and Fishin' Jimmy is found, alive but badly injured, at the foot of a steep, rocky ledge on the mountain. He had slipped on the rocks while rescuing the dog. Fishin' Jimmy is carried back to the Profile House, where he dies, sorry that he has saved a dog instead of a soul, but satisfied nonetheless.

Fishin' Jimmy appeared initially in the Princeton Review. Prime, a Princeton graduate with strong ties to the university, was probably responsible for this. Then the story was published as a book, which sold many copies both here and abroad. Slosson went on to write many other stories set in the Franconia region. Most of the stories had a religious theme. For example, *Aunt Randy* tells the story of a simple Franconia woman whose faith is strengthened through her love for butterflies and other insects. *White Christopher* focuses on an albino boy who identifies with the snow cross that forms on Mount Lafayette in the springtime. These and other stories were well received, but Slosson's most popular work would always be *Fishin' Jimmy*.

In 1905, William Prime died, and Annie Trumbull Slosson began to lose her interest in the mountains. She sold the Mount Lafayette House in 1908 and invited a niece and her family to use Gale Cottage. Although Slosson stopped going to the White Mountains, she continued writing and collecting well into her eighties. At her death in 1926, Gale Cottage was willed to her niece. Today, Annie Trumbull Slosson's family is still enjoying this historic summer home.

Other memories of Prime and Slosson can still be found in Franconia Notch. After William Prime passed away, William Bridge's widow owned Lonesome Lake for a while. Then she sold it to the owners of a hotel in Franconia Notch, who used the cabin as a destination for donkey trips that brought hotel guests up to the lake. When the State of New Hampshire bought the land for the Franconia Notch State Park in 1929, Lonesome Lake and the surrounding property, including the cabin, were part of the purchase. The State immediately leased the cabin to the AMC, and in 1930, after adding a kitchen and dining area, the AMC opened the cabins as the newest addition to its hut system.

That same year, the AMC cut a new trail—over two miles in length—to connect Lonesome Lake with the Kinsman Ridge Trail near Kinsman Pond. The club's Committee on Nomenclature thought long and hard about a name for the trail. Finally, they decided to call it the Fishin' Jimmy Trail after the character from Annie Trumbull Slosson's best-known short story.

The Lonesome Lake cabins served as an AMC hut until the 1960s, when they were torn down and a new hut was constructed on the other side of the lake. The clearing where William Prime's cabin once stood can still be seen today.

6: The Explorers

F EW EXPERIENCES in hiking and mountaineering can compare with the thrill of exploring an unfamiliar region or reaching a summit that no one has ever stood on before. Today, exploration and first ascents are usually associated with inaccessible parts of the world. But just a little over a century ago, the romance of finding the unknown was still possible in the White Mountains.

By 1870, the White Mountains had become one of the most fashionable vacation areas in America, yet, incredible as it might seem, much of the region was still a pathless wilderness. In a vast area between the Ammonoosuc River on the north and the Sandwich Range on the south, many mountains had no names, even more had never been explored, and any number of waterfalls and ponds were just waiting to be discovered. Looking back on this period years later, one writer recalled that "the forest glens of New Hampshire were, some of them, almost as little known of men as valleys of the Caucasus or the Himalayas."

A major effort to learn more about the "forest glens of New Hampshire" began in the winter of 1876 when a group of men who shared an interest in mountains attended a meeting at the Massachusetts Institute of Technology and formed the Appalachian Mountain Club (AMC). The new organization set itself the task of systematically exploring the White Mountains and opening them up for hiking. That spring, L.F. DePourtales, the AMC's first Councillor of Exploration, drew up a list of thirteen localities that needed to be explored. He encouraged AMC members to visit those places, keep journals of their trips with compass courses and estimates of distances, draw profile views of mountains "wherever practicable", and, if possible, use a barometer to measure heights.

Women, who had been admitted to the club at its second regular meeting, participated in the AMC's exploring work from the
beginning. Of these pioneering women, six stand out for their
dramatic accomplishments. Three were from the same family—
Edith Cook, Lucia Cook Pychowska, and Marian Pychowska. The
other three were Suzie M. Barstow, Isabella Stone, and Martha F.
Whitman.

LUCIA PYCHOWSKA, MARIAN PYCHOWSKA, AND EDITH COOK

The year is 1872. The place: a rugged area to the north of
Shelburne, New Hampshire. On a bright summer day, a party of
four is climbing a pathless mountain. In the lead is Eugene
Beauharnais Cook, a lean, wiry man who is forty-two years old.
Following closely behind are three women in ankle-length skirts:
his younger sister, Edith Cook; his older sister, Lucia Cook
Pychowska; and Lucia's daughter, Marian Pychowska. At age
twelve, Marian is already an experienced wilderness explorer.

At a time when most White Mountain tourists were content to
spend their vacations visiting famous sights such as the Flume and
the Profile, the Cooks and Pychowskas could frequently be found
deep in the woods, tramping through thick brush in search of the
unknown wonders of the region. They were among a select few who
took pleasure in exploring the backcountry in the early 1870s.

Each member of the Cook and Pychowska families contributed significantly to the AMC effort to explore the White Mountains, but theirs is primarily a group story. With Eugene Cook
usually in the lead (he had an "almost unerring divination of the
best route to reach an end," according to Lucia and Marian), the
Cooks and Pychowskas covered more un-trod ground in the White
Mountains than almost anyone else in the last quarter of the nineteenth century. They were also key figures in the great path-building endeavors in and around the northern peaks of the Presidential
Range in the 1880s.

Considering their background, one might have expected to find the Cooks and Pychowskas relaxing on the veranda of one of the grand hotels instead of beating their way to the summit of an unexplored mountain. Lucia, Eugene, and Edith Cook grew up in Hoboken, New Jersey, where they enjoyed a privileged life in a handsome residence that offered views across the Hudson River to New York City. Eugene and Edith remained single all their lives, but Lucia married John Pychowski, a distinguished Polish musician and composer. Marian Pychowska was their only child. After their marriage, Lucia and her husband lived with Eugene and Edith in the family home.

With two servants attending to their needs, the Cooks and Pychowskas were able to spend their days in gentle cultural pursuits. Each family member had many special talents: Eugene Cook was an authority on chess and figure skating and the author of a book on each subject; he was also a skilled violinist. Both Lucia and Marian had a gift for writing and translating. Lucia contrib-

Lucia Pychowska (left) and Marian Pychowska (right) were exploring the backcountry of the White Mountains well before the AMC was founded.

uted articles to *Catholic World* and translated books from French to English. Edith Cook also wrote, but, more importantly, she was a talented artist who produced many fine drawings and paintings depicting the scenery and wildflowers of the White Mountains. All three women had a keen interest in botany and were experts at identifying the region's ferns and flowers.

Every summer the whole family packed up and went to the White Mountains for two or three months. Throughout most of the 1870s, they vacationed near Shelburne, New Hampshire, a town along the Androscoggin River, and they spent their time roaming all over the rugged territory to the north and east. The only family member who did not participate was John Pychowski. He remained back at the inn, working on his musical compositions.

Many of the peaks the Cooks and Pychowskas investigated were part of the formidable Mahoosuc Range, including Bald Cap, Goose Eye Mountain, and Mounts Carlo and Success. While exploring the range, if they came across a mountain or pond that lacked a name, they created one. They left "numerous unique and attractive names as their gift to those who were to come in their footsteps," wrote Frank H. Burt in an *Appalachia* article about White Mountain nomenclature. Some of the names they chose were definitely unique. For example, the Cooks and Pychowskas named Mount Carlo, thereby immortalizing a dog that sometimes accompanied them on their explorations. On one occasion they spent several days looking for an elusive waterfall that some local innkeepers had told them about. When they finally came upon the waterfall, they decided to call it Lary's Flume after one of the innkeepers. Along the way, they also discovered and named Dry-Ad Falls (this play on the word "Druid" was chosen because the waterfall was often dry), Gentian Pond, and Moss Pond, features now familiar to hikers on the Appalachian Trail.

The family members began their exploring several years before the AMC was founded. The Cooks and Pychowskas were skeptical when they first heard about the new club, looking upon the members as "suspicious intruders" and jokingly calling them "Apes." But they soon realized the "Apes" were nice people who shared their interest in exploring, and they joined the club and became active participants. One of Lucia and Marian's first contributions as AMC members was to write about their mountain investigations around Shelburne. Lucia and Marian jointly produced a paper on Bald Cap, and Marian wrote about their ascents of Mount Ingalls and Goose Eye Mountain. The papers were read at an AMC field meeting and submitted for publication in *Appalachia*, the club's outstanding journal. These were the first of several articles the women would write about their explorations.

In 1878, the family spent its summer vacation at the Goodnow House in Sugar Hill, a village near Franconia Notch. A fellow guest was Isabella Stone, a twenty-eight-year old woman from Framingham, Massachusetts. That fall, Isabella Stone and the Cook and Pychowska women began exchanging letters, although Isabella and Marian, an articulate nineteen-year old by this time, did most of the letter writing.

Their correspondence lasted for eight years. Fortunately, Isabella, a careful and methodical woman, saved the letters she received along with drafts of some of the letters she sent and portions of her diary. All of this material somehow survived down to the mid-twentieth century and was eventually sold at auction to collectors with an interest in White Mountain history. In 1995, Peter Rowan and June Hammond Rowan published *Mountain Summers*, an edited collection of the letters that presents a captivating picture of the women's adventures in the mountains.

Today, when people are frequently on a first name basis within seconds of meeting, it is surprising to read the letters and realize that for four years Marian and Isabella always began their letters with "Dear Miss Stone" and "Dear Miss Pychowska." They must have been just as formal when they were together, for in 1882, when Marian finally opened a letter with "Dear Isabella," she added, "You see from my non-conventional greeting that I have more courage on paper than when face to face."

If they were timid in this respect, the women were clearly daring in the wilderness, especially Edith Cook and the Pychowskas. The letters give detailed accounts of their outings and depict them plunging fearlessly into thick forests and virtually dashing up mountains, beating today's "book times" by a considerable amount. Dura Pollard, a guide whom Isabella hired, had also been out with the Cooks and Pychowskas. Isabella wrote to say that Pollard was amazed at their speed on the trail, remarking, "Never seed ladies go like them, they never stopped to rest...."

Marian frequently commented on the pleasures of bushwhacking in her letters. "It was delightful to be in pathless woods once more and to struggle with as fine a growth of hobble bush as we have ever seen," she wrote. On another occasion, she described a trip that required crossing a thick belt of stunted trees, declaring, "Such a bout with the tough dwarfs is exhilarating...."

Following their stay in Sugar Hill, the family spent the next three summers in Campton, a village along the Pemigewasset River. The AMC was doing lots of exploring in the area, and at first the Cooks and Pychowskas joined in enthusiastically. But eventually, Lucia and Marian grew restless, for there wasn't enough to do. In late 1881, Marian wrote Isabella and mentioned a plan to stay somewhere else the next summer:

> The south side of the mountains in general is so well explored by "Apes" and others, that this, among other reasons, makes my mother and myself turn our eyes secretly to the north side once more, secretly because the others are so satisfied with the Pemigewasset Valley. We dare do no more than whisper to one another of a change.

Marian and Lucia plotted through the early part of the winter before making their proposal to the other family members in February. They suggested trying the Ravine House, an inn in Randolph, New Hampshire, that had been recently opened by the father and son team of Abel and Laban Watson. The inn was located within easy reach of the northern peaks of the Presidential Range and looked across to King Ravine, which Marian described as "one of the grandest things in the region."

The Cooks and Pychowskas were the first guests to arrive at the Ravine House in the summer of 1882. The next to come was a retired Chicago businessman named William Peek. A pleasant, scholarly man, Peek immediately became a friend and companion on their outings. Laban Watson was completing a trail to the top of Mount Madison (the Watson Path), and the Cooks and Pychowskas and William Peek pitched in to help. Soon they were making plans for other mountain paths.

That summer marked the beginning of a virtual explosion of trail building activity in the northern Presidential Range and the hills behind Randolph. During the rest of the decade, more than fifty miles of new paths would be opened. In her letters to Isabella, Marian frequently described whole days spent measuring a new path or placing signs or scouting a possible new route to a moun-

The Ravine House in Randolph, New Hampshire, was the center for a group of pathmakers who, in the 1880s, built over 50 miles of new trails in the northern peaks of the Presidential Range and the hills behind Randolph.

tain summit. She also wrote that she was working on a map of the northern slopes of Mount Madison because the existing ones were "so deplorably wrong."

Other Ravine House guests were caught up in the excitement as well. Strong friendships grew out of this shared devotion to path building as the same people returned to the inn year after year to spend part or all of the summer climbing and working on trails. George Cross, one of the Ravine House group, wrote about this golden era in an *Appalachia* article:

> There was little lounging on the piazza in good weather in the old days. Early in the morning everybody in costumes as simple as they were suitable, with a not cumbersome lunch in a paper bag, armed with bill-hook or hatchet, measuring tape and compass, set out for the mountains. Everybody, under the inspiration and guidance of Mr. Peek or Mr. Cook or Madame Pychowska, became path finders and path makers. We counted that day lost whose low descending sun saw no new waterfall discovered, no new paths pushed many rods through the scrub, no new view cleared of brush to wider prospect. In the evening, in the parlor circle, we reported and enlarged upon our works, discussed and named our discoveries. The names were always significant and felicitous, because Mr. Peek was the final arbiter in such matters.

When they were not making new paths, the Cooks and Pychowskas continued their exploring. Their guide was a "Table of the Less-Visited Peaks of the White Mountains" that had been published in an early issue of *Appalachia*. It listed forty-seven peaks, and members were asked to visit them and supply detailed descriptions. Eugene Cook served as the AMC's Councillor of Exploration from 1883 to 1885, and when he took office, thirteen of the Table's forty-seven mountains remained to be investigated. By the end of Cook's term, all had been climbed and studied.

The women participated fully as Eugene Cook carried out his duties. Edith Cook was a member of a party that first explored the entire Moriah and Carter Range, a prelude to opening it up by means of an AMC path. Marian explored Mount Wildcat and traveled through Evans Notch where she climbed Mount Royce and North and South Baldface. The women prepared accounts of all these expeditions for *Appalachia*. Family members also investigated the region behind Randolph—Mount Crescent, Mount Randolph, the Ice Gulch, and the Pond of Safety.

In letters to Isabella, Marian described some of their exploring methods. When the women were on the summits of mountains, they spent a lot of time looking at other mountains to find out what lay behind and in front of the various peaks. This was important because the maps were inaccurate, and in many areas, the relations of the mountains to one another were not clear to anyone. Edith Cook's skill as an artist was particularly helpful, for she could make drawings that depicted the outlines of the mountains and showed their geographic connections.

When they visited new areas, the women sometimes climbed trees to get views. Isabella was so impressed by their ability to do this in long skirts that she asked Marian about it in a letter. Marian replied:

> You wonder how my aunt and I climb trees. Consider first that the middle sized spruces were conveniently branched down to the ground. The getting up is very easy as the skirts come naturally after. A graceful descent is more difficult, as the same skirts are apt to remain above, but my uncle and Mr. Peek considerately left us, so that grace did not have to be considered.

In 1884, Marian Pychowska and a fellow Ravine House guest named S.M. Barstow were investigating the top of Huntington Ravine on Mount Washington when they climbed down to a "long overhanging knife blade of rock," a feature known today as the Pinnacle. They may have been the first to discover this precipice, which is well known to modern-day rock and ice climbers. Two years later, when Marian led a group that included the famous guide Charles Lowe and several AMC leaders to the Pinnacle, she learned that it was new to all of them.

In the summer of 1885, Eugene Cook was finishing the last of the "less-visited peaks," and the women elected to spend their time in more sedentary activities. Writing to Isabella, Marian said she was "taking it easy this summer, and leaving the big things to the men." She did assist by measuring some new paths, but her mornings were spent translating "a little book of piety" that had been given to her by a French priest.

The next year, Marian wrote Isabella several long letters giving a detailed account of an AMC field meeting at the Mount Washington Summit House. And then the correspondence ended. The last letter—or at least the last one existing today—was written by Marian in October of 1886, shortly after the family returned to Hoboken from the mountains. A few months later, Marian, a Roman Catholic, entered the Monastery of Saint Dominic in Newark, New Jersey. She spent the rest of her life as a cloistered nun. Known as Mother Mary Saint Peter, she eventually moved to Cin-

A group of trampers gathers in front of the Ravine House. Eugene B. Cook is the fifth person from the right.

cinnati, Ohio, and founded that city's Monastery of Saint Dominic. She died there in 1942 at age eighty-two.

It is uncertain whether Lucia Pychowska or Edith Cook continued their exploring and path-building for no record exists of their activities in the White Mountains after the late 1880s. However, Eugene Cook spent at least part of every summer at the Ravine House and was an active path maker into the early years of the twentieth century.

The family members (with the exception of Marian) lived in Hoboken until the end of their lives. Edith Cook died in 1902 at age sixty-three, Lucia Pychowska died three years later at age seventy-nine, and Eugene Cook passed away in 1915 in his eighty-fifth year.

Eugene Cook is remembered in the Cook Path, which leads from the Randolph Hill Road to the Ice Gulch, a boulder-strewn area with many caves that contain perpetual ice. The AMC established the Marian Pychowska Award in honor of this extraordinary young woman who did so much to make the White Mountains known and accessible to others.

SUZIE M. BARSTOW

In Marian Pychowska's letters, S.M. Barstow is referred to simply as Miss Barstow. Her full name was Suzie M. Barstow, and she was in her late forties when she and Marian visited the Pinnacle. A resident of Brooklyn, New York, Barstow studied art in the United States and Europe. Returning to a studio in Brooklyn, she settled down to a career as a painter and art teacher. She specialized in landscape painting and exhibited her works at the National Academy and at the Pennsylvania Academy.

An AMC member, Barstow took part in some of the club's explorations. She joined Edith Cook, Eugene Cook and several others when they traversed the entire Carter-Moriah Range, and she visited Imp Mountain and wrote a description of it for *Appalachia*.

Barstow was also an extremely active climber. In fact, Suzie Barstow may have been the original woman "peak-bagger" in the White Mountains and the Adirondacks. An article entitled "Fair Mountaineers" in an 1889 issue of *The White Mountain Echo* gives a lengthy description of a Brooklyn artist, a "Miss B____" who was too modest to allow her name to be mentioned. It was clearly Miss Barstow. The article said that "Miss B____" had "climbed...all the principal peaks of the Catskills, Adirondacks and White Mountains, as well as those of the Alps, Tyrol and Black Forest, often tramping twenty-five miles a day, and sketching as well, often in the midst of a blinding snow-storm." The number of mountains she had climbed numbered one hundred and ten. Marian also documented Barstow's climbing accomplishments in a letter to Isabella, reporting that Miss Barstow had climbed seventeen mountains during a month's stay in Waterville.

ISABELLA STONE

White Mountain historians owe a great debt to Isabella Stone, who so carefully preserved her correspondence with Marian and Lucia Pychowska and Edith Cook. These letters give a memorable picture of the early years of the AMC and the exhilaration that was experienced as the club members explored the unknown regions of the White Mountains.

Mary Isabella Stone was born in 1850 in Concord, New Hampshire, but her family moved to Framingham, Massachusetts, when she was still an infant. Isabella, who never married, lived in Framingham for the rest of her life. She described herself as a middle-aged spinster in her letters, yet she was in her late twenties and early thirties when she wrote them.

Beginning in her childhood, Isabella spent many summers in the White Mountains. Even as an adult, she frequently went on vacation with her parents, and they seem to have watched over her closely. For example, they objected to some of her climbs, fearing they would be too dangerous. When Isabella wanted to climb Loon Pond Mountain, an outing highly recommended by Marian,

Isabella Stone

her father spoke with the guide and investigated the safety of a river crossing before allowing her to go. After climbing Mount Adams with Charles Lowe as guide, Isabella longed to ascend nearby Mount Madison as well. But she decided against it, explaining in her diary, "There would be time enough to climb it, really, but I prudently refrain to please mother."

After meeting the Cooks and Pychowskas, Isabella continued to spend her vacations at the Goodnow House and other inns in the western part of the White Mountains. Although she did not see much of the Cooks and Pychowskas after their initial meeting, she followed their suggestions on mountains to climb and kept in touch about their mutual efforts to build paths and open up the mountains.

Isabella contributed significantly to the path-making in and around Franconia Notch. Her first project involved opening a trail to Bridal Veil Falls, a graceful waterfall on the side of Cannon Mountain. Some AMC members wanted a path to the falls, and Isabella took charge of the project, raising money and obtaining permission from landowners so people could pass over their land. Displaying a clear talent for organizing, Isabella carried out the work "with great energy," according to a note in *Appalachia* praising her for her work.

In the early 1880s, while staying in North Woodstock, Isabella explored nearby Harvard Brook to its source. The brook featured a lovely cascade known as Georgianna Falls. She paid to have a path cut to it; then she measured the entire route and put up signs that she had prepared herself.

For a long time she had a "cherished scheme" to open a route from North Woodstock to Mount Bond. The path she proposed approximates the Wilderness and Bondcliff Trails of today. Isabella persuaded people who lived around North Woodstock to contribute time and money to the cause, and she approached the AMC Councillor of Improvements as well. Unfortunately, Isabella abandoned the project because of an illness, and the path did not become a reality until many years later.

Isabella also took part in some AMC explorations. Her companion on many exploring trips was George Russell, the owner of the Russell House in North Woodstock, where Isabella stayed for part of several summers. She described Russell as a "quiet, slow, plain, honest-hearted farmer" and "a sober family man of over fifty years." Her parents were well acquainted with Russell and had no objection when Isabella went on outings with him as her only companion. Would they have allowed it if they had known that Russell confided in her, speaking of his "past trials and future plans," or if they had realized that Isabella was quite fond of her farmer companion? Being a proper Victorian lady, Isabella kept her true feelings hidden, but her diary entries suggest her feelings for George Russell went deeper than friendship.

During Eugene Cook's term as Councillor of Exploration, one of the mountains on the "Table of Less-Visited Peaks" was Mount Waternomee, located near Mount Moosilauke. Isabella and George Russell decided to explore it. Even finding Waternomee proved to be a problem. Osgood's guidebook said it was in one place, and the state map put it in another. "For further knowledge it became necessary to go on to both these Waternomees, and also to look down upon the whole from the summit of Moosilauke," Isabella explained in an *Appalachia* article. She and Russell determined that Waternomee was "one long mountain, extending nearly north and south for almost four miles, with four crests separated by but slight depressions." They determined which peaks were which and where they stood in relation to other nearby mountains. It was "rough work," requiring a bushwhack "over rocks, prostrate logs, moss-covered pitfalls, and through thick underbrush."

In 1885, Isabella, who never enjoyed robust health, suffered from a curious illness characterized by loss of appetite, sleeplessness, and general debility. Her doctor ordered her to avoid any mental effort or worry and even suggested that she give up letter writing. Isabella spent part of the summer convalescing at the Russell House. She was a guest there when she wrote her last letter to Marian in July of 1885.

Little is known about Isabella Stone's life after the correspondence with the Pychowskas and Edith Cook ended. Despite the mysterious illness that so restricted her activities, Isabella lived for many more years and passed away in 1921 at the age of seventy-one.

MARTHA F. WHITMAN

Another woman who helped lift the veil of mystery surrounding the mountain region was M.F. Whitman or Martha Fairfield Whitman, a resident of Lexington, Massachusetts. Marian

Pychowska met Whitman at an AMC field meeting and described her to Isabella in a letter written in September of 1882:

> She is a person of about thirty-five, evidently very independent, but ladylike and unassuming. I think she is the most thoroughly good lady mountaineer I have ever seen, short and stout and therefore somewhat scant of breath, but energetic and untiring....Miss Whitman's dress, when I saw her, was a dark blue flannel down to her boot tops and a rather long half fitting sack belted in, relieved with a little white trimming.

Marian's guess about Martha Whitman's age was off by seven years. Born July 13, 1840, Whitman would have been forty-two when Marian wrote her letter. Like Marian, Whitman had spent many summers in the White Mountains. Well before the AMC was established, Whitman visited the mountains with the Lexington Botanical Club, a group composed of four women and two men. The club members usually stayed in comfortable inns, but as tourism grew and people filled the hotels, they decided to try camping out in the wilderness. The experiment was such a success that they began doing it each summer. The club camped throughout the White Mountains and even went as far north as Dixville Notch and Lake Umbagog.

Whitman joined the AMC soon after its founding and immediately turned one of her White Mountain experiences into an article for *Appalachia*. "A Climb through Tuckerman's Ravine," published in the third issue of the journal, is a hair-raising story of a climb that almost ended in tragedy. On a day in mid-August, Whitman and a gentleman friend set off at two in the afternoon to see the snow arch in Tuckerman's Ravine. After reaching the floor of the Ravine, they lost their way among a grove of alders, and then, to compound their problems, a storm came up and heavy rain began to fall. Deciding that their best course of action was to press on to the summit of Mount Washington, they began to climb. As soon as they reached the top of the Ravine, the storm hit them with such force they had to "cling to each other for support."

Uncertain if they were heading in the right direction, Whitman and her companion continued to climb and were relieved when they stumbled over some stones and found themselves on the Crawford Bridle Path, a landmark familiar to them. Following the path, they inched their way up the summit cone "sometimes on foot, often on hands and knees." As they reached the end of the Bridle Path, Whitman's companion reminded her that Lizzie Bourne had perished even closer to the summit. Somehow, they dragged themselves over ice-covered boulders and made it to the warmth and safety of the Summit House.

In another issue of *Appalachia*, Whitman contributed an article entitled "Camp Life for Ladies" in which she extolled the delights of camping and advised women on proper clothing, the intricacies of constructing hemlock beds, the danger from bears (nonexistent), and other matters.

An enthusiastic explorer, Whitman took part in several White Mountain exploring trips including one of the most exciting and difficult expeditions undertaken by the early AMC members—a traverse of the Twin Mountain Range. A long ridge that serves as a boundary of the Pemigewasset wilderness, the Twin Range features a series of peaks bearing the names North Twin Mountain, South Twin Mountain, Mount Guyot, Mount Bond and Bondcliff. The views from the latter three peaks are regarded as being among the finest in the White Mountains. Some AMC members had observed the Twin Range from higher mountains, most notably Mount Lafayette, and were eager to explore it, but the summits proved hard to reach, and the few who tried came back with discouraging reports.

Nonetheless, in August of 1882, Augustus E. Scott, the AMC's Councillor of Improvements, resolved to make another attempt to explore the range. As he wrote in *Appalachia*, he wanted to determine "the feasibility of a path over the ridge, or to some of its summits, and to mark the route."

Scott could not find any men who wished to join him and had decided to undertake the journey with a woodsman who had some familiarity with the region. But shortly after Scott announced his plans, he received an unusual letter. A prominent gentleman from Bethlehem wrote to say that Charlotte Ricker, a special correspondent for *The White Mountain Echo* wanted to know if any ladies would be on the trip. If women were going, Ricker, who had "much experience among the mountains" according to the letter-writer, wanted to be a member of the party.

Scott answered immediately, explaining that the exploration would be so arduous that no men were willing to accompany him, and it had never occurred to him to ask a woman. Then he added, "half in jest," that he was always ready to assist women who liked to explore wild places, and if Miss Ricker could endure the hardships (which he described in detail), he would "invite the only lady I know for whom the undertaking is feasible" to come along. He soon received a reply saying Ricker definitely wanted to go on the exploration. Scott talked with the woman he had in mind for the trip, and she agreed to go. Then he happened to read Ricker's letter to a third woman and was astonished when she asked to join the group too.

"I was fairly caught," Scott later reflected. "I had painted the probable difficulties of the proposed exploration in glowing colors, and had rather disdainfully expressed a willingness to invite ladies to accompany me if they dared attempt it; and here were three ladies who not only dared, but were eager to go. I would not retract, although I had many misgivings, and some doubts of their reaching even the first summit."

Scott hired another packman, and the party of six met about two miles north of the Twin Mountain House on a day in early August. As they set out on their expedition, the two woodsmen—a 60-year-old guide named Allan Thompson and a young man named Odin—led the way. Both looked very smart in new embroidered shirts. The ladies followed, and Scott brought up the rear. It was the beginning of a seven-day journey that would take them across the Twin range, then down the valley to the east branch of the Pemigewasset River and on to Thoreau Falls and Crawford Notch.

Two accounts of the trip were eventually published. A three-part series by Ricker appeared in *The White Mountain Echo* in late August and early September of 1882 under the title "The Wilderness: Wild Places and Rugged Peaks First Visited by Woman." Ricker's articles presented an exciting, somewhat melodramatic chronicle of their adventure. Scott produced a more sober report that was read at an AMC meeting the following March and subsequently published in *Appalachia*.

Although both descriptions of the trip are filled with fascinating detail about the expedition, neither Scott nor Ricker gave the names of the other women members of the party. Ricker identified them as "two Boston ladies, one of whom has hitherto accomplished much in the way of tramping...." Scott described the women as a medical student and a doctor of medicine "who is happy in escaping for a few days a wearisome city practice."

Two sources confirm that one of the women was Martha Whitman. In a letter to Isabella Stone, Marian Pychowska commented on Ricker's newspaper articles and mentioned that Whitman had participated in the Twin Range exploration. Whitman is also identified as a member of the exploring group in a brief article in *Among the Clouds*. According to this article, the other woman was Dr. Laura M. Porter of Boston. Porter, who joined the AMC sometime in 1880 or early 1881, was the doctor of medicine mentioned by Scott, and Martha Whitman was the medical student.

The first day of the exploration was uneventful, for the party went only as far as the foot of North Twin. The next day they began climbing, and after scrambling over some steep ledges, they encountered an immense sea of impenetrable scrub that soon had them "floundering helplessly." Moses Sweetser's *Guide to the White Moun-*

tains had warned that the Twin Mountain peaks were difficult to reach "owing to the stunted growth near their tops," but the reality exceeded anyone's expectations. Scott termed the scrub "indescribable" and left it at that. Ricker also said it was impossible to depict this "villainous undergrowth," yet she attempted a description:

> Twin Mountain scrub is a growth of spruce varying in height from six feet to six inches. Much of it is more than a century old, and has grown tough and ragged and gray by exposure to the blasts of the long cold New Hampshire winters. It is knitted and interwoven, tree with tree, branch with branch, as if each section were a part of some vast and intricate web. There is no one way that you can meet and defy this pitiless enemy—unless you pause to hew it from your path. Is it of average height, with a small interstice at the bottom? You must crawl under it. Is it short and tangled? You must make it your footstool. Is it knit tightly from top to bottom? You must fight your way through its unbending branches. It will scratch you mercilessly, it will aim for your face, your hands, your person; it will make voyages of discovery in your eyes, will entangle your feet, will push aside your hat, and relentlessly Absolomize you. You may force it down—it will assert itself just in time to give you a parting thrust. Vainly will you search for favoring inlets and outlets.

Somehow they persevered. When the party finally reached the summit of North Twin, there was "almost a mutiny for the possession of the pint canteen of water." Although they had hoped to go on to the summit of South Twin, their thirst forced them to change plans and descend into a ravine in search of water. They finally located a trickle late in the day and had no choice but to camp overnight among some rocks.

Water problems plagued the exploring party repeatedly in the first days of their trip. Today, most hikers know the importance of carrying plenty of water and food, and they stop on the trail frequently to drink and eat snacks. The members of the Twin Mountain expedition carried only a one-pint canteen of water for six people. They relied on springs and streams in the valleys that offered clear, pure water, but when they followed routes along ridgelines, water was unlikely to be found.

On the third day, after a battle with more scrub, they reached the summit of South Twin Mountain and were rewarded with a magnificent view. Ricker was thrilled to be a member of the first group of women to ascend the mountain. As she wrote in her *Echo* article:

> I am well nigh exhausted, but the scene outspread before me is of such exceeding glory and magnitude, and there is such an exultation in the thought that I, a woman, unused to privation and fatigue, have reached a height found unattainable by stalwart men because of the difficulties to be encountered by the way, I forget for the moment that I am suffering from pain and thirst and weariness....

At this point, Scott must have been having doubts about Ricker's claim of "much experience among the mountains." He noted that Ricker and the packmen were showing "evident signs of demoralization—the new, embroidered shirts have long ceased to be attractive, and the flannel dress of the latter is torn to shreds...." By contrast, he described Whitman and Porter as looking "fresh."

After leaving the summit of South Twin, the party became separated and spent the night apart. Ricker and Odin, who were in one group, were carrying all the food. They dined sumptuously, while the others had nothing but two sticks of chocolate to be shared among four people. Although this was Whitman's and Porter's only food after a hard day of tramping, Scott observed that both women were "merry and enthusiastic" the next morning.

Fortunately, everyone was soon reunited, and on the fourth day, they climbed Mount Bond and explored Bondcliff. It was extremely hot and everyone's thirst was acute. "Our lips crack and the skin peels from the roofs of our mouths," Scott wrote. However, the views from Bondcliff into the unlogged Pemigewasset Wilderness were of such unsurpassed beauty that they remained there an hour before descending to the valley floor, making their camp, and finding some much-coveted water.

Their hardships decreased once they had completed the traverse of the Twin range. The thick underbrush was minimal, and the exploring party had plenty of water as it followed the northerly branch of the Pemigewasset River toward Thoreau Falls. Yet Ricker was so weary she decided to go out to Crawford Notch by a shorter route. The packmen accompanied her to be sure she made it safely. Scott, Whitman and Porter completed the trip as planned, finishing their seven-day outing with a difficult climb up the pathless backside of Mount Field and then over Mount Willard.

In her final *Echo* article, Ricker paid tribute to Whitman and Porter's impressive performance: "Fatigue, privation and exposure necessarily attend exploration, and to the endurance of these hardships few ladies are equal. Those accompanying the survey on this trip are exceptional women, and possess powers of endurance to which many men are strangers."

Augustus Scott had hoped to determine the feasibility of a path across the Twin Range, and the expedition proved it would be a worthy undertaking. The next summer, AMC members, including Augustus Scott and Martha Whitman, repeated the Twin Mountain trip, traveling over a newly cleared AMC trail.

By the summer of 1884, Whitman had finished her medical studies and was working as a resident physician, probably in Boston. She died in December of 1884 of unknown causes. Marian Pychowska commented on Whitman's death in a letter to Isabella, saying, "I have most pleasant memories of this good lady."

In the early 1890s, the AMC Councillor of Exploration announced that places "of special interest in the White Mountains are now nearly all explored, and members are of necessity turning their attention elsewhere." Those members who loved the challenge of discovering the unknown began investigating some unexplored mountains in the American West. Others focused on a new mission—preserving the White Mountain forests so that future generations could enjoy them.

7: The "Spark Plug of Wonalancet"

CONSIDERING THE White Mountains' long history as a popular tourist area, it is not surprising that some of the region's most memorable women have been associated with inns or hotels. Two women in the hotel business—Dolly Copp and Sarah Hayes—have even had the distinction of having geographic features named for them. Both Dolly Copp and Sarah Hayes are remembered because they were warm and personable—and in Dolly Copp's case, because she was a character. Another woman innkeeper, Katherine Sleeper Walden, is remembered not only for her personality but also for her work to build trails and protect the mountains.

KATHERINE SLEEPER WALDEN

Of all the women innkeepers in the White Mountains, no one affected the area in which she lived more profoundly than Katherine Sleeper Walden, owner of Wonalancet Farm in Wonalancet. This slight, blond-haired woman virtually resurrected this village at the foot of the Sandwich range and transformed it into a lively summer and winter resort. She also helped protect the nearby mountains as part of the newly established White Mountain National Forest. Katherine Sleeper Walden exerted such a vital influence on the community that one resident later described her as the "spark plug of Wonalancet."

Born in the Boston area in 1862, Katherine Sleeper lost her mother when she was ten, and she and her father then went to live with his parents. Her grandfather was a well-known Bostonian who held various political posts and served as editor of *The Boston Journal*. Kate, as she was called, had a traditional upbringing, and given her family background, she quite naturally turned to the newspaper business as a young woman and worked for a time as a reporter.

Not much else is known about Kate Sleeper's life until 1890 when she went to Tamworth, a village in the southern part of the White Mountains, to recuperate from an illness. While convalescing at a boarding house in town, she decided to try running an inn by herself. She was going on twenty-eight at the time, although she told everyone she was younger. (She was "by tradition eighteen years old," wrote Marjory Gane Harkness in *The Tamworth Narrative*.) Perhaps she chose to forget a few years because during her visit to Tamworth she met an attractive man who was almost ten years her junior—Arthur Walden, the fun-loving, adventurous son of a distinguished Boston minister.

The two immediately became friends, and Arthur began driving Kate around as she looked for a suitable house to buy and turn into an inn. One day they visited Birch Intervale, a hamlet located a few miles outside Tamworth. Although it had once been a thriving small community with farms, sawmills and a bobbin mill, Birch Intervale had fallen on hard times and was unofficially known as Poverty Flats. Not much was there except an old chapel and some rundown homes. However, something about the village fired Kate's imagination, and she announced, "This is where I'm going to live!"

Before long, Kate and Arthur came upon an old 1814 farmhouse situated on over six hundred acres. A hill with a view of the Sandwich and Ossipee Ranges rose up behind the house, and a lovely cascading brook flowed through the property. Arthur thought the house and land were ideal, but Kate worried that the land was more than she could manage. She wanted to run a comfortable, well-appointed inn where guests would eat home-grown vegetables and have butter and milk supplied by a dairy located right on the premises, but these were ambitious plans, difficult for one woman to carry out alone. Finally, she told Arthur she would buy the farmhouse if he would run the farm, and he agreed to do so.

Kate spent the winter of 1890-1891 enlarging and renovating the house. When spring came and the snow melted, revealing a

Wonalancet Farm opened in the summer of 1891. Guidebook writer Moses Sweetser described it as "a capital summer boarding house."

trash-filled yard, some men in the neighborhood came and cleaned everything up without any prompting from Kate. Later, one of Kate's friends, Jean Roff Smith, would cite this incident as an example of Kate's genius for winning people over and making them want to help her: "All her life she possessed the rare quality of inspiring others to want what she wanted," Smith wrote.

The inn, which she called Wonalancet Farm, opened in June of 1891. Within a year, Moses Sweetser included it in his *Guide to the White Mountains*, describing the inn as "a capital summer boarding house, with its 650 acres of meadows and ravines, forests and brooks, and the beautiful Wonalancet Falls."

Kate Sleeper needed some way to attract guests, so that first summer she invited Charles Fay, a founder and past president of the AMC, and another club officer to Wonalancet Farm to talk to local residents about opening up the nearby mountains for climbing. On an evening in late August, a small group of people gathered at the inn where they heard Fay describe the AMC's trail work in other parts of the White Mountains. Turning to the hiking possibilities around Birch Intervale, Fay suggested that a path be cut from the village to the top of Mount Passaconaway and urged residents to form an association to maintain the path and develop other trails as well.

A few days later, the AMC leaders joined with a party of farmers to clear out an old logging road that led from a decaying sawmill known as Dicey's Mill up to the top of a ridge; from there they cut a path to Mount Passaconaway's summit. The path, which is known as the Dicey's Mill Trail, is still the most popular route up the mountain.

Kate Sleeper's influence on Birch Intervale was just beginning. Over the next few years, the villagers cleaned up their yards, repaired the roads, and restored the old chapel, giving it a new tower and bell. She was the moving force behind all of these improvements. She also worked to have a post office established in the community and served as the first post-mistress. When the Postal Service requested that Birch Intervale change its name to avoid confusion with Intervale, the small village near North Conway, she came up with Wonalancet, the same name the poet Lucy Larcom had bestowed on a small mountain in the village decades earlier.

The formation of a trail association, first suggested by the AMC leaders, took a bit longer to accomplish. In 1898, Kate organized the Wonalancet Out Door Club (WODC), and, under her direction, it immediately became a vital, active group. A 1901 WODC guidebook detailed the organization's accomplishments in its first three years: "Paths have been cut, guide boards placed, a camp built on Whiteface, trees planted along the highway to provide shade in future years, and a sketch map of the roads and paths made for public use." Ten years earlier, no trails had existed in the Wonalancet area. By 1901, club paths led to the summits of Mounts Whiteface, Tripyramid, Passaconaway, Wonalancet,

*Katherine Sleeper Walden. She wore a cord around her
waist, from which she hung the keys to the rooms in her
inn.*

Hedgehog, Paugus and Square Ledge, and a path connected
Waterville Valley and Albany Intervale.

Arthur Walden was not around during the early days of the
WODC. He had run Kate's farm for several years, but, being restless and eager for adventure, he went off to Alaska in 1896. He
stayed there for two years, made a brief visit home, and went back
for the gold rush. He returned to New Hampshire for good—or
at least for a good many years—in 1902. As soon as he arrived
home, he asked Kate to marry him. She agreed, and they were
married that year in a gala wedding at Wonalancet Farm.

For the better part of the next three decades, they would manage Wonalancet Farm together. As an innkeeping team they had
no equal: Kate, the charming, determined organizer, and Arthur

(or Wally as his friends knew him), a raconteur in the tradition of Ethan Allen Crawford. Instead of telling bear stories, Arthur Walden enthralled guests with tales of his adventures in Alaska and the Yukon.

In the first decade of the twentieth century, Wonalancet Farm was one of the few inns or hotels to promote winter sports. At first, Arthur and Kate Walden encouraged snowshoe parties. The camp that the WODC built on Mount Whiteface was furnished with a stove, which made it a good destination for winter climbers. Later, sled dogs were introduced and became a popular winter diversion. During his years in the Far North, Arthur Walden had used sled dogs to haul goods and had come to appreciate their superiority as a means of transportation over snowy terrain. In the winter of 1909-1910, he took four mixed-breed St. Bernard puppies; named them Rud, Yard, Kip, and Ling; and trained them to pull a dog sled that he had built himself. This was the first dog team in New England, and it immediately proved its worth by hauling material for the building of a new hydroelectric plant deep in the woods. The dogs also contributed greatly to the pleasure of inn guests and village residents. As Marjory Harkness wrote, "This team was an utterly delightful innovation in the intervale at that time, and every girl or woman given a ride in the sled had the thrill of her life."

Years later, Walden would own a dog named Chinook, which became the most famous dog in America. The product of a Husky mother and half-breed St. Bernard father, Chinook led teams to victories in races around New England, and he accompanied Walden when he went on Admiral Richard Byrd's first expedition to Antarctica in 1928.

After slightly more than two decades in the White Mountains, Kate Walden could take pride in many accomplishments. The inn was thriving, and under her leadership, Wonalancet had become one of the best climbing and winter sports centers in the White Mountains. However, her most significant triumph came in 1914 when she set out to save a beautiful tract of wilderness land encompassing 5,600 acres in a secluded valley between Mount Whiteface and Mount Passaconaway. Known as the Bowl, the land had never been logged and included some fine stands of virgin spruce. Although the Bowl had no trails, many hikers had been there and knew of its beauty. From her earliest years in Wonalancet, Kate had concerns about this tract of land, concerns that had to do with changes taking place in the lumber industry.

Logging had been going on in the White Mountains from the days of the first settlers, and trees were always cut freely without any regard for the future. No one worried much about this because the timber supply seemed so plentiful. Around 1870, however, a method was developed for making paper from wood pulp instead of rags. The primary tree for making wood pulp was spruce, which grew abundantly in New Hampshire, especially on the high, steep slopes of the mountains.

The pulp industry was somewhat slow to get going, but by the 1890s, it was in high gear. To get at the spruce, the loggers attacked the mountainsides, cutting everything in sight. Philip Ayres of the Society for the Protection of New Hampshire Forests (SPNHF), a group established in 1901, wrote a series of articles in *The New England Magazine* under the title "Is New England's Wealth in Danger?" This is how Ayres described the loggers' methods:

> The high slopes are slashed over in a manner so recklessly wasteful, that from one third to two thirds of the total forest cover, all of the small trees are felled and left on the ground, prostrate and dead, cut merely to remove more easily the few trees of larger size. This mass of debris invites fire, which almost invariably follows....

To haul timber out of the mountains, a network of logging railroads had been constructed, and sparks and hot coals from the engines ignited some of the fires. Careless hikers, who dropped a match or failed to completely stamp out a campfire, caused others. Forest fires became an all-too-common occurrence, and the loss was enormous. In the spring of 1903, extensive fires demolished 84,000 acres in the White Mountains—more than a tenth of the region. In some areas, fire annihilated all the vegetation and even the soil leaving nothing but barren rock. In 1907, a lightning strike on the east side of Owl's Head Mountain set fire to acres of slash left from a clear cut. The fire spread rapidly and burned for over a week, destroying extensive acreage on the sides of Mounts Bond, Garfield, Guyot and Lafayette.

This devastation alarmed many people, but they felt helpless to do anything about it for the land was all privately owned. The federal government did not own a single acre of land in the White Mountains and neither did the State of New Hampshire. Ironically, in 1867 the state had sold all of the publicly owned land in the region for scandalously low prices.

In 1907, a fire that began on Owl's Head Mountain destroyed about 35,000 acres of forest.

Beginning in the last decade of the nineteenth century and continuing through the first decade of the twentieth century, various dedicated individuals and groups, most notably the AMC and the SPNHF, waged a vigorous campaign to pass legislation giving the federal government the power to set aside lands in the Eastern United States as national forests. One bill after another was introduced into Congress, but many politicians were skeptical about the idea of the government purchasing private land, and the bills were always defeated.

Finally, Congressman (later Senator) John W. Weeks of Massachusetts championed the cause. Although he represented Massachusetts, Weeks was a native of Lancaster, New Hampshire, a town in the White Mountain region, and he was keenly aware of the need to protect the forests. Under his dynamic leadership, a bill finally passed both the House and the Senate, and President Taft signed it into law on March 1, 1911. The new law, known as the Weeks Act, asserted the federal government's interest in the headwaters of navigable rivers and gave Congress the authority to spend money to acquire private land to protect watersheds. The Weeks Act has provided the basis for all of the national forests in the eastern half of the United States.

The Weeks Act established a National Forest Reservation Commission and gave it the authority to determine what lands the government should buy. At its first meeting, the commission decided to spend its initial appropriation of $200,000 on land in the Southern Appalachians and the White Mountains. In 1912, the federal government acquired about 30,000 acres, most of it located on the northern slopes of the Presidential Range. Thus the White Mountain National Forest was born.

The government purchased more land in the next year and a half, so that by 1914 almost 140,000 acres had been put into National Forest. Meanwhile, the lumber companies were logging as fast as they could, hoping to keep a step ahead of the federal government as it bought up land. Kate Walden and other Wonalancet residents knew that the Conway Lumber Company, one of the largest landowners in the White Mountains, owned the Bowl. They also knew that the company was planning to begin cutting trees in the Sandwich range, and they feared that the Bowl would be logged.

One day in 1914, Louis Tainter, vice president of the Conway Lumber Company, called at Wonalancet Farm to see Arthur Walden on a business matter. As Tainter was about to leave, Kate caught him at the door and asked if he would give her a sixty-day option on three thousand acres "up there" for fifty thousand dollars. Without even requesting time to think about the proposal, Tainter signed an agreement on the spot.

With her option in hand, Kate Walden immediately telephoned Marjory Gane (later Harkness), and the two women went to work. They wrote a letter to the Forest Service in Washington making a bold proposal: If the residents and friends of Wonalancet raised $25,000, would the government provide matching funds to purchase the Bowl? The Department of Agriculture, which oversaw the Forest Service, replied that the minimum tract of land they would purchase had to be 20,000 acres. A tract of just 5,000 acres was too small.

This response, although discouraging, did not stop the two determined women. As Marjory Gane Harkness recorded in *The Tamworth Narrative*:

> It was our good fortune that Senator Gallinger of New Hampshire happened to be on the Forest Reservation Commission. He probably heard of Wonalancet for the first time, but now he heard of it in every mail. Senator Weeks was reached, and correspondence started flowing to our Congressmen. Edgar Rich, Wonalancet neighbor then general counsel of the powerful Boston & Maine Railroad, threw himself into the campaign with ardor; certain Concord magnates bestirred themselves; all absentee summer owners were made acquainted with the hovering danger. Offers of help and money mounted rapidly. To record

grass roots feeling, a petition was circulated around as far as horse and buggy on bad roads would carry it. This alone took time; only men's signatures were useful at that period, which increased difficulties in seeking names. Passing a house or a barn being built was a stimulus, for then a dozen good carpenters would lengthen the list.

Initially, Senator Jacob Gallinger thought the price for the Bowl was much too high and refused to cooperate. But the grass roots effort in Wonalancet had its desired effect, and Gallinger began working to persuade his colleagues on the Forest Reservation Commission to include the Bowl in the White Mountain National Forest. Eventually the lumber companies came down on their price, and the government purchased the Bowl without any help from residents of Wonalancet. The tract was part of an 85,000-acre purchase by the federal government announced in September of 1914. Today, the Bowl is part of the Sandwich Range Wilderness and is treasured as one of the few remaining old-growth forests in the Northeast.

Arthur and Kate Walden continued to run Wonalancet Farm until the early 1930s. They had seen many changes over the years, particularly with the advent of the automobile, which had changed the pattern of tourism in the White Mountains. When automobiles became the preferred mode of transportation to the mountains, people did not spend long vacations in one spot anymore, and many inns suffered from the loss of business. The Great Depression seriously affected the inn business as well. Deciding that the time had come to retire, the Waldens leased Wonalancet Farm and moved to Brook Walden, a nearby summer cottage that had originally been owned by Arthur's father.

In March of 1947, an oil burner caught fire in Brook Walden. Although Arthur Walden managed to get Kate to safety, he went back into the house to fight the fire and never came out. Kate later commented that Arthur "went as he would have liked to go, in a glory of flame." Kate died two years later at age eighty-six.

Kate and Arthur Walden are buried on either side of a granite boulder on the small lawn of the Wonalancet Chapel.

Arthur Walden is remembered in the Walden Trail, a route up Mount Passaconaway. Kate Sleeper Walden is memorialized in several geographic sites: Mount Katherine, a small hill in the village of Wonalancet, has been named in her honor. Her name was also given to the Kate Sleeper Trail, which connects Whiteface with Mount Tripyramid via a double-domed ridge. This ridge is known as Sleeper Ridge and the domes are known as East Sleeper and West Sleeper.

8: The Mountaineers

I N THE 1920s, several young women from New England be
gan making a name for themselves as skilled mountaineers. Most
of these women learned to climb at places fairly close to home—
at the Quincy Quarries near Boston, for example, or the cliffs and
gullies of the White Mountains in New Hampshire and of Katahdin
in Maine. After this apprenticeship, they journeyed to the European Alps, the American and Canadian Rockies, and other high
places of the world. In a brief period of about twenty years, they
achieved many notable ascents, and one of them, Miriam O'Brien
Underhill, earned a reputation as the greatest woman climber the
United States had ever produced.

The women, who knew one another and frequently climbed
together, shared similar backgrounds. Most were either born in New
England or brought up in the region. All were well-educated, and
most spoke several foreign languages—an asset for climbing in foreign countries. All loved the outdoors and spent lots of time in the
White Mountains. When they were not climbing mountains, they
could often be found shooting rapids in canoes or trying another
sport new to most Americans—skiing.

They were not the first American women to scale high mountain peaks. At the turn of the century, two women who also hailed
from New England—Fanny Bullock-Workman and Annie Smith
Peck—made mountaineering history with their extraordinary climbs.
But Bullock-Workman and Peck climbed primarily on ice and snow,
and they were always accompanied by men. By contrast, the young
women climbers of the 1920s and 1930s ascended towering rock
walls, relying on precise balance and small toe- and finger-holds to
achieve their objective. At first, the young women climbed with men,
but then some of them realized that they were missing out on one

of the joys of mountaineering—leading a route. So, first they tried guideless climbing, and then, after gaining proficiency and confidence, they undertook "manless" ascents.

Why did these New England women take up mountaineering at this time? Part of the answer is that after World War I, women everywhere were breaking down barriers and engaging in new pursuits. And mountaineering was one pursuit that became much more feasible when the restrictive dress code for women began to change. In 1915, when Miriam O'Brien was seventeen, she climbed Mount Washington with a classmate and the classmate's father and younger sister. O'Brien remembered that the younger sister wore bloomers, but she and her friend felt skirts were "more seemly" because they were older. "But that was about the beginning and end of the skirt period for me," O'Brien later wrote. "Trousers for climbing and skiing were just coming into fashion about the time that I needed them."

Women in long dresses and showshoes climb a steep slope in the White Mountains around 1900.

Miriam Underhill in the Alps in 1932. By the 1930s, women were wearing trousers and even shorts for hiking and climbing.

Also, the women were young when rock climbing as a sport was just getting started in New England. Europeans had been doing roped climbing for many years, but no one tried it in the Northeastern United States until 1916. Curiously, two men took up the sport that year, and neither one knew of the other's activities. A man named John Case, who had climbed in the European Alps, took some rope and used it on some cliffs in the Adirondacks. Meanwhile, Frank Mason, a Boston businessman, decided to try rock climbing.

MARGARET HELBURN

The first New England woman to take up rock climbing was Margaret Mason Helburn. Born in 1889, Margaret was the daughter of Frank Mason, the man who initiated the rock climbing movement in New England. An active AMC member who served as president of the club in 1918, Mason enjoyed hiking, and he nurtured a love of the outdoors in his daughter that would remain with her all her life.

Any woman who climbs major mountains has something within that pushes her to seek new challenges. Margaret probably acquired this drive in her childhood. When she was twelve, her mother died and she was given responsibility for running the household as well as the care of a two-year-old sister. Later, Margaret's son Nicholas Helburn would speculate that "this experience undoubtedly contributed to her independent spirit and perhaps to her unconventional ways."

After earning a degree in social work from Simmons College, Margaret married Willard Helburn, an avid outdoorsman whom she had met on the trail. In 1914, the Helburns moved to Salem, Massachusetts, where Willard had a leather manufacturing business. The great Salem fire occurred in 1914, and Margaret, who always had a keen interest in helping others, took charge of an effort to provide clothing for people left homeless. She was only twenty-five at the time, but she handled the job well and this further enhanced her confidence and encouraged her independence.

Not long after Margaret and Willard Helburn were married, Frank Mason introduced them to rock climbing. Mason had become intrigued by the sport after reading about it in a British series entitled *The Badminton Library of Sports and Pastimes*. He got some rope and began climbing—first with his family, then with some friends—on rocky outcrops near Boston. Some of his favorite spots were the West Roxbury cliffs and a field of glacial erratics near Salem known as the Peabody Boulders.

Margaret Helburn took to rock climbing immediately. Although she was a mother by the time she took up climbing, that did not slow her down. As her sister Dorothy Mason Fuller wrote in an *Appalachia* article, Margaret began "scaling peaks in the Alps and Dolomites between babies," and developed into "one of the foremost women climbers in the United States." Nicholas Helburn recalled that his mother liked to boast to male friends that she

Margaret Helburn with her guide, Armand Charlet (center). According to Nicholas Helburn, Margaret's son, this was "her favorite picture of herself, reminding her on into her nineties of how active and competent she had been."

had climbed Mont Blanc under conditions they could not match. When the men took umbrage, Margaret would blithely explain, "I was pregnant."

Margaret and Willard Helburn also broke new ground as winter climbers. They did much of their climbing with a group of experienced winter hikers known as the Bemis Crew. The group originated in 1923 when the Helburns gathered some friends for a week of vigorous winter climbing in the White Mountains, using the Bemis Place, an inn in Crawford Notch, as their base. Everyone had such a good time that the group decided to meet every year in February. Although they met at different locations, they continued to call themselves the Bemis Crew.

During their annual gatherings, the Bemis Crew roamed all over the Presidential Range and ascended many of the White Mountain peaks over 4,000 feet high. They frequently dealt with powerful winds and steep, icy conditions—excellent training for summer climbing in the Alps. Years later, the members of the group compared notes and discovered that more than half had climbed the Matterhorn.

Although, Margaret and Willard Helburn were pioneering rock and ice climbers in the White Mountains, little information is available about their activities after the late 1920s. However, their children have fond memories of trips to the White Mountains as they grew up, and Nicholas Helburn said that "they trained their four children and many of their friends' children in mountaineering skills including rock climbing."

MARJORIE HURD

Marjorie Hurd also learned rock climbing under Frank Mason's direction. A Boston native, Hurd was a bright, strong-minded woman who graduated from Radcliffe College in 1909 and then studied law at the Portia College of Law. She spent most of her career as an attorney with the Boston Legal Aid Society. In 1925, she and a few others asked Frank Mason to help them train for an AMC summer trip to the Alps. Mason gave them excellent instruction, and that summer Hurd and the others reached the summits of such famous peaks as the Matterhorn and the Jungfrau.

Later, writing about the origin of AMC rock climbing for *Appalachia*, Hurd reported that everyone on the trip "returned full of enthusiasm" for climbing and began searching for places in New England where they could practice and develop their skills. The

Marjorie Hurd in the Alps

AMC *Bulletin* for April 1926 carried the first notice of a rock climbing outing, according to Hurd, and although just a few climbs
were scheduled that year, by the spring of 1927 "a weekly schedule was in full force."

Hurd emerged as a leading force in Boston rock climbing circles
and climbed extensively in the White Mountains, the Katahdin
region, the American Rockies and the European Alps. A member
of the first Bemis Crew gathering, Hurd also enjoyed winter climbing, and she excelled at white water canoeing.

ELIZABETH KNOWLTON

Elizabeth Knowlton acquired her love for the outdoors on
childhood visits to the White Mountains. Born and raised in

Elizabeth Knowlton in the 1950s. Knowlton climbed major mountains on four continents.

Springfield, Massachusetts, Knowlton was the daughter of Marcus Knowlton, the Chief Justice of the Massachusetts Supreme Court. Her mother, Rose Ladd Knowlton, enjoyed hiking and began taking Elizabeth to the White Mountains when she was seven. Even as a child, Knowlton realized that she liked climbing and that just being in the hills brought joy to her life.

Knowlton graduated from Vassar College in 1916 and took a year of graduate work at Radcliffe College. Then she headed off to the Canadian Rockies and the Selkirk Mountains of British Columbia where she made her first major climbs.

During the early 1920s, Knowlton joined the AMC and soon became a valued member of the rock climbing committee. A freelance writer, Knowlton served as secretary of the committee and one of her jobs was to send out notices about outings. Years later, Robert Underhill (an accomplished mountaineer and Miriam Underhill's husband) remembered that Knowlton produced notices that "had a real kick. She could write things up that really got people to come on our trips."

Like the other New England women mountaineers from this period, Knowlton used the White Mountains as a training ground for ascents in other parts of the world, including South America, Europe, Canada, and Asia. In 1932, she was the only woman member of the German-American expedition to Nanga Parbat in the Himalayas, the world's seventh highest peak. Although she did not attempt to reach the summit, she climbed to a camp at 20,000 feet and remained there for a month so she could send news dispatches about the expedition's progress to *The New York Times*. Knowlton described her Himalayan experiences in the beautifully written book *The Naked Mountain*.

JESSIE WHITEHEAD

Although she was a native of Cambridge, England, the colorful Jessie Whitehead deserves to be included with this group. The daughter of mathematician Alfred North Whitehead, Jessie Whitehead came to the United States when her father joined the Harvard faculty in the mid 1920s. She settled in Cambridge and worked as a cataloger at one of the Harvard libraries, where her skill in Arabic languages was an asset. A witty, pipe-smoking eccentric, Whitehead joined the AMC soon after arriving in this country and became an avid climber.

Whitehead participated in many AMC rock climbing trips, and in 1928 she was part of a group that pioneered a challenging route on the Pinnacle in Huntington's Ravine. Over the next few years, she used her rock climbing skills to ascend mountains in the Canadian Rockies and the European Alps.

Other women climbers who honed their climbing skills in the White Mountains were Avis Newhall, Florence Peabody, and

Christine Reid. In the late 1930s, Reid was the first woman to climb Mount Columbia in the Canadian Rockies. She also excelled at skiing and pioneered in filming ski techniques and ski races.

MIRIAM O'BRIEN UNDERHILL

Miriam O'Brien (later Underhill) was the most outstanding of all the women mountaineers from this period. She was also one of the last to take up serious climbing. Born in Forest Glen, Maryland, O'Brien grew up in Dedham, Massachusetts, a suburb of Boston. Her father edited a Boston newspaper and her mother was a physician, one of the first women to graduate from the Boston University Medical School.

Miriam spent childhood summers at her maternal grandparents' home in Lisbon, New Hampshire, a town to the west of Franconia Notch. During these visits, her mother took her on many climbs in the White Mountains, and Miriam acquired her first interest in mountain adventure and a love of wild, uncrowded places. In 1914, when Miriam was sixteen, she went to the European Alps with her mother and her younger brother Lincoln, and the three returned there several times in the early 1920s. On all of these trips, O'Brien climbed mountains, but they were simple ascents, the sort of climbs undertaken by beginners. "I cannot understand why I was so slow in getting started," O'Brien wrote in her autobiography *Give Me the Hills*.

The spark she needed came during the winter of 1925-26 on some trips to the White Mountains and Katahdin. The day after Christmas in 1925, Miriam, her brother Lincoln, and two male companions left the AMC's Pinkham Notch Camp at eight in the morning and hiked up to Huntington Ravine, the steepest glacial cirque on Mount Washington. Miriam and one man wore snowshoes, while her brother and the other young man were on skis. Heavy snow made trail breaking difficult, and by the time they reached the floor of the ravine, it was mid-afternoon. Everyone realized it was important to head for home before darkness set in, but the skiers, who were equipped with crampons and ice axes, decided it would be quicker and more enjoyable to climb up the steep Huntington headwall and then ski down the Auto Road. Unable to dissuade them from continuing, Miriam and the man on snowshoes returned to the Glen House, where everyone was staying, arriving in time for dinner.

As the evening wore on and the skiers failed to return, Miriam became worried. A party set out to look for the young men, but O'Brien was the only one equipped with snowshoes, and because the snow was deep, she climbed up to the ravine alone. She reached the base of the Huntington headwall about midnight. "Strangely enough, it turned into one of the most glorious experiences of my life," she wrote in *Give Me the Hills*. In the full moon, she could see the tracks that her brother and his friend had left in the snow and ice, which told her that they had reached the top of the headwall. Relieved, she gazed at the beautiful winter scene around her. It was "a magical world of diamonds. In the gorgeous moonlight every snow-frosted rock, every sugared twig, every ice-sheet on the majestic walls above, every frost feather, sparkled and glittered." She lingered for a few minutes and then headed back to the Glen House where everyone was reunited.

O'Brien said the experience gave her a tremendous "boost towards becoming a real mountaineer." From her midnight climb, she had learned an important lesson: that she was capable of more than she realized. Although she had been exhausted when she first returned to the Glen House, she had not noticed any fatigue when she set out again to search for the two young men. "I have been, in my lifetime, extremely tired more than once," she wrote. "I have been too tired to eat, too tired to sleep. But I don't remember any occasion when I couldn't have walked another mile if my life had depended on it."

Another boost came in February of 1926 when Margaret Helburn, whose father and stepmother knew Miriam's mother, invited O'Brien to join the Bemis Crew on a weeklong trip to the

White Mountains. The Bemis Crew, which gathered at the Glen House that year, spent the week hiking and climbing on the Carter-Moriah and Presidential Ranges. O'Brien felt she "must have passed some sort of test" because at the end of the week, the Helburns asked her to join a small group going to Katahdin in Maine in early March.

When they set out for Maine from Boston's North Station, Margaret Helburn introduced O'Brien to the other people in the party. One of the men she met was a Harvard philosophy instructor, Robert L.M. Underhill. "That name will come up again," she hinted coyly in *Give Me the Hills*.

That week they climbed a long, steep gully known as the Chimney and ascended Elbow Gully in the North Basin. They also crossed the Knife-Edge, a narrow serrated ridge with a formidable reputation among summer hikers. In winter, its ice-covered rocks made for "real alpine going," according to Miriam.

The events of the winter stimulated O'Brien's appetite for some serious climbing in the Alps. The Bemis Crew and the people on the Katahdin trip, especially the Helburns, helped by giving her the names of the best guides and describing the plans she should make in advance. And thus in May of 1926, Miriam O'Brien sailed for Europe, determined to become a rock climber.

O'Brien started in the Dolomites and hired the renowned Antonio Dimai as her guide. Dimai had two sons, Angelo and Giuseppe, and one or the other usually came along on climbs because of O'Brien's inexperience. She was fortunate to learn under three men with remarkable skill, especially Angelo Dimai, who was unusually graceful on rock.

That summer, she developed into an excellent climber, so proficient that she would "dazzle the mountaineering world with her exploits," as the talented British climber Dorothy Pilley wrote in her autobiography, *Climbing Days*.

Some of O'Brien's most outstanding climbs took place in the Mont Blanc region around Chamonix. In 1927, she and Margaret Helburn, with Armand Charlet as guide, were the first women to ascend the Grepon by the Mer de Glace face. The Grepon is one of the famous Chamonix aiguilles, sharp rocky spires rising up from the basin of the Mer de Glace glacier. In 1881, the renowned British climber A.F. Mummery had tried and failed in his attempt to climb the Grepon from the Mer de Glace side. Another British mountaineer, Geoffrey Winthrop Young, finally pioneered this route in 1911. Sixteen years later, it was still considered one of the most difficult climbs in the Alps. In addition to being the first women to make this climb, O'Brien and Helburn were the first people to accomplish it in one day without a bivouac.

The next year, O'Brien and Robert Underhill traversed all five points of Les Aiguilles du Diable in one long eighteen-hour day. The points had all been climbed separately, but no one had ever done all five in one outing. Another of Miriam O'Brien's impressive climbs was the ascent of the Finsteraarhorn by the northeast face. The Finsteraarhorn is found in the Bernese Oberland, an area of Switzerland featuring many world-famous peaks including the Jungfrau, Monch and Eiger. Only two parties (in 1904 and 1906) had ever ascended the sheer northeast face of the Finsteraarhorn, and both had required a bivouac. In 1930, O'Brien and her guide Adolph Rubi completed their climb in one thirteen-hour day.

Initially, O'Brien always climbed with a licensed guide, but before long, she decided she wanted to do guideless climbs. She gave her reasons in her book:

> Very early I realized that the person who invariably climbs behind a good leader, guide or amateur, may never really learn mountaineering at all and in any case enjoys only a part of all the varied delights and rewards of climbing. He has, of course, the glorious mountain scenery, the exhilaration of physical acrobatics, the pleasure that comes from the exercise of skill, and these acrobatics often require skill to a considerable degree. But he is, after all, only following.

The one who goes up first on the rope has even more fun, as he solves the immediate problems of technique, tactics and strategy as they occur. And if he is, as he usually is, also the leader, the one who carries the responsibility for the expedition, he tastes the supreme joys. For mountaineering is a sport which has a considerable intellectual component. It takes judgment to supply the ideas, to make wise and proper decisions on the route, the weather, the possibility of danger from stone-fall, avalanche, concealed crevasse, etc., and above all, to know what one's own capabilities permit.

As she thought about guideless climbing, O'Brien realized that if women were really to lead and be responsible for a climb, no men could be part of the party. For if even one man were along, he would be likely to "spring to the front and take over" in an emergency. With this in mind, she decided to try some manless as well as guideless climbs.

As a first step, she organized a trip with a competent male assistant. In September of 1928, O'Brien and George Cachat, a Chamonix porter, traversed the Grepon. With O'Brien in the lead, they climbed to the north end of the summit ridge, went over five or six pinnacles until they reached the south end of the ridge, and then descended to the Col des Nantillons. The steep granite walls fell away 3,000 feet on one side of the ridge; on the other side, the drop-off was 5,000 feet. In *Climbing Days*, Dorothy Pilley recorded the leading mountaineering journal's reaction to O'Brien's achievement:

> The *Alpine Journal* wavered between incredulity and stern disapproval, announcing the first woman's lead of the Grepon with a hesitating "it is reported" and declaring that "Few ladies, even in these days are capable of mountaineering unaccompanied."

The next year O'Brien accomplished her first truly manless climb—an ascent of the Aiguille du Peigne with British climber Winifred Marples. Three days later, she and Alice Damesme, an

*Miriam Underhill on a traverse of the Mittelgruppe of the
Engelhorner. Photograph by Adolph Rubi.*

outstanding French climber, completed the first manless traverse
of the Grepon. In *Give Me the Hills*, O'Brien described the climb,
explaining that she and Damesme set out from the Montenvers
Hotel around half past two in the morning. When, three hours
later, they arrived at a standard breakfast spot for climbers, the
men assembled there were amazed when they learned what the
two women were planning to do. "They were too courteous to

laugh at us outright, but we did intercept quite a lot of sideways glances and barely-concealed smiles. Alice and I pretended not to notice," she wrote.

The climb went smoothly, and by mid-morning the two women were on the large flat rock that forms the actual summit of the Grepon. All went well on the descent, and by early afternoon they were safely back at the place where they had breakfasted. O'Brien, who delighted in the male reaction to her manless exploits, reported that in Chamonix that evening one man groaned, "The Grepon has disappeared. Of course, there are still some rocks standing there, but as a climb it no longer exists. Now that it has been done by two women alone, no self-respecting man can undertake it. A pity, too, because it used to be a very good climb."

In 1930, O'Brien began the season by joining Marjorie Hurd on a manless ascent of the Torre Grande in the Dolomites. Next, she set her sights on the Matterhorn. Although it was not as difficult as the Grepon, the Matterhorn was a celebrated peak, and for that reason O'Brien wanted to add it to her list of manless climbs. She could not make any attempts that year, but in the summer of 1931, O'Brien, Alice Damesme and Jessie Whitehead spent the better part of August trying to climb the world-renowned mountain on the Swiss-Italian border. Although they tried repeatedly and came fairly close to the summit on one climb, bad weather always forced them to turn back. Each time the women went up to the Matterhorn Hut, which is 5,500 feet above Zermatt, they rode on mules O'Brien's mother had hired so they could save their strength for the actual climb. After their fourth trip up to the hut, Whitehead, with characteristic wit, said there was "not a mule in Zermatt that didn't recognize her." Finally, the women decided the weather was not going to cooperate that season and abandoned their efforts.

The next summer, matters were different. Jessie Whitehead was climbing in the Canadian Rockies and the Selkirks and was unavailable for another attempt on the Matterhorn, but O'Brien and Damesme went to Zermatt on August 12 and found the weather ideal. "The next day we climbed the Matterhorn. It was as easy as that," O'Brien declared in *Give Me the Hills*.

Some friends from the Groupe de Haute Montagne (an elite section of the French Alpine Club) had prepared a reception in Chamonix to honor the women for being the first of their sex to climb the Matterhorn alone. O'Brien skipped the celebration and went to the Eastern Alps to join Florence and Dean Peabody and Robert Underhill for some climbing. The Underhills were married in early 1933, and as she wrote, "After that, for nineteen years, my constant companion on every climb was Robert Underhill. Manless climbing is fun for a while, but this other arrangement is better!"

By the late 1930s, the era of these outstanding women mountaineers was coming to an end. In the winter of 1940-41, Elizabeth Knowlton made some first ascents in the Sierra Nevada de Santa Marta Range in Colombia. Writing about her trip in *Appalachia*, she said, "Last winter when we found it possible to attempt some first ascents in South America, we decided to seize the opportunity. For it might well be one's last chance for such an adventure, in these sad and troubled times." Knowlton was right. Less than a year later, the United States was at war, and travel was restricted. For the rest of the decade, American women climbers would stay closer to home.

As the women mountaineers grew older and were no longer making astonishing first ascents, many of them continued to find joy in the mountains. And for Miriam Underhill, the White Mountains, the region where she had first learned to love hills and wild places, would be the scene of some new accomplishments.

During the war years, the Underhills began spending summers in Randolph, New Hampshire, a center for many climbers and path makers over the years. Eventually, they moved to Randolph permanently to be able to get into the hills more often. During the 1950s, Miriam began taking close-up pictures of the White Mountain wildflowers in their natural settings and at various stages in their life cycles. Her son Robert later described her as a pioneer in this kind of nature photography. As an outgrowth of this interest, Miriam spearheaded an effort to develop a guidebook of alpine flowers. In 1964, the AMC published *Mountain Flowers of New England*, which featured some of Miriam's color photographs.

The Underhills also took up the idea of climbing mountains over 4,000 feet high. Nathaniel Goodrich, Dartmouth College librarian, had suggested the idea for the White Mountain Four Thousand Footer Club in an article in the December 1931 issue of *Appalachia*. After describing the practice of European climbers to climb all the sixty-seven Alpine peaks of at least 4,000 meters and the rush to climb 14,000-foot peaks in Colorado and all Adirondack peaks of 4,000 feet or more, Goodrich wrote, "It occurred to me that it might be amusing to try this game on the White Mountains." A few people proceeded to climb all the peaks in the White Mountains that were 4,000 feet or higher (Goodrich had identified thirty-six; the correct number is forty-eight), but the White Mountain Four Thousand Footer Club was not officially formed until 1957. The Underhills, who had been climbing in the White Mountains for years, had no difficulty gaining membership. They simply had to add a few peaks like Owl's Head, a remote mountain that few people would climb if it were not slightly over 4,000 feet high. Miriam and Robert Underhill were among the first to qualify for membership in the club, and Miriam was the first woman member.

After becoming charter members of the White Mountain Four Thousand Footer Club, the Underhills came up with the idea of climbing the four-thousand-footers during the winter. Miriam thought this would be "an even more sporting challenge than ambling up the well-trodden trails in summer." She considered the difficulties: In winter, finding the trail is harder. There is less time for resting because the days are shorter. Necessary supplies make the rucksack heavier. Finding water is a problem, and the water and food often freeze. And, most important of all, breaking trail in deep snow can be extremely hard work. "All these may sound like splendid arguments for staying home, but not to us," she wrote in *Give Me the Hills.* "We were old winter climbers from way back, thanks to the good old Bemis Crew...."

Because they made up the game, the Underhills were able to set the rules, and they decided "winter" meant the true calendar period between December 20 and March 20. Both Miriam and Robert had already climbed about half of the White Mountain four-thousand-footers in the winter, although they had not always done the same ones. They set out to complete their list of unclimbed mountains, and in December of 1960, when they reached the summit of Mount Jefferson, their final winter peak, they became the first members of the White Mountain Winter Four Thousand Footer Club.

Miriam Underhill (center) at the 1965 dedication of the AMC's Mizpah Hut.

Robert Underhill was seventy-one, and Miriam was sixty-two. Notably, the Underhills did these winter climbs when they had to break the trail by themselves. Today's winter climbers have an easier time; they frequently walk on trails packed down by the parties that have preceded them.

Before long, Miriam participated in two other games: climbing all the peaks in New England that were at least 4,000 feet high, and ascending the one hundred highest mountains of New England. Miriam Underhill joined the New England Four Thousand Footer Club as a charter member in 1965.

That same year, while working on the "hundred highest," she made what she described as "a great big careless mistake which was to cause much worry and work to so many people." It was September, and she and a companion, Louise Baldwin, were climbing Elephant Mountain in Maine when they lost their way. The mountain lacked a trail to the top at the time, and the women chose a compass course that followed the county line, taking them across the Appalachian Trail and, after a difficult bushwhack, up to the summit ridge of Elephant. On their descent, they took a slightly different route, intending to pick up the Appalachian Trail again and then walk out to their car. However, the Appalachian Trail was not heavily used in 1965, and Underhill and Baldwin completely missed it. After searching and searching for the trail, they came to a small clearing and saw that Elephant Mountain was "an astoundingly long distance away." It was then that they realized they were in trouble.

The women spent the night in the woods (in a temperature that hovered around 50 degrees, fortunately) and finally found their way out to a road late the next afternoon. Initially, no one in the passing cars was willing to stop for them. "Perhaps Louise and I were too unpractised at hitchhiking, or perhaps we were too 'unwashed,' as some of the newspapers later observed," Underhill speculated in an account of her adventure published in *Appalachia*.

This newspaper photograph depicts Miriam Underhill (left) and Louise Baldwin (center) with the motorist who picked them up after they lost their way on Elephant Mountain.

Eventually, a resident of Bethel, Maine, who had just heard about the lost women on his car radio, picked them up. By then, a major search effort was underway, and stories about the two women were printed in newspapers across the country. One friend even wrote to Underhill, saying that she had heard about their misadventure from a Spanish radio bulletin from Mexico City.

Despite her experience on Elephant Mountain, Miriam Underhill had remarkably few mishaps during her mountaineering career. She fell just once, climbing the Central Gully of Huntington Ravine with the Helburns. They had chosen a route that went across a small waterfall, and the force of the water swept her down the gully. Fortunately, Willard Helburn's rope held her, and she was unharmed.

Only one other women climber from this group had a severe accident. Jessie Whitehead's mountaineering career ended in 1933 after she had a near-fatal fall while ice climbing in the Odell Gully in Huntington Ravine. Whitehead was still drawn to the mountains, however. She built a cabin near Mount Chocorua and continued to hike, snowshoe and ski.

All of the New England women climbers loved mountains for their own sake as well as for the joy of physical adventure. As Miriam Underhill wrote in *Give Me the Hills,* " …when you have spent in the hills most of the time you have for recreation and pleasure, they come to mean much more than just the fun of acrobatics. The most urgent desire, after an illness or an absence, is to climb a mountain again. And in occasional times of strain just to walk in the hills brings a strengthening of the spirit, a renewed courage and buoyancy."

Mountains gave meaning to these women's lives and probably contributed to their good health. Although mountaineers routinely face danger and hardship, as a group they tend to have an enviable record of longevity. Consider these women: Miriam Underhill, the youngest of the climbers, died in 1976 at age seventy-seven. Marjorie Hurd died a year later, a few months shy of her ninety-first birthday. The year 1980 saw the passing of Margaret Helburn, age ninety-one, and Jessie Whitehead, age eighty-six. Elizabeth Knowlton outlasted everyone, passing away in 1989 at age ninety-three.

9: A White Mountain Original

THE WHITE MOUNTAIN region has always had its share of characters. In *Chronicles of the White Mountains*, Frederick Kilbourne devoted a whole chapter to them. He described such notable eccentrics as John Nazro, who claimed to own the summit of Mount Washington and tried to collect tolls from everyone who visited, and "English Jack," who spent his summers living as a hermit in Crawford Notch and who earned money by selling souvenirs and a booklet containing his life story.

Although Kilbourne probably did not know it, by 1916, the year he published his book, an extraordinary woman had made her appearance in the White Mountains. Her name was Emilie Klug and she would become one of the most famous White Mountain characters of the twentieth century.

EMILIE KLUG

A native of Germany, Emilie Klug lived in the United States for many years and worked as a nurse in Brooklyn, New York. From approximately 1912 until the mid-1930s, she spent her summer vacations wandering around the White Mountains completely alone. She was an engaging character—a warm-hearted, ever-smiling woman with an abiding love for the mountains.

Emilie's unusual appearance and curious habits combined to make her a legend. Her typical hiking garb consisted of woolen knickers, a heavy woolen skirt, a flannel shirt with large pockets, and a soft, shapeless hat. She wore heavy, hobnailed boots and always carried a walking stick. Although her pack was small and usually filled with books, Emilie had devised various ways to carry the items she needed for her three- or four-week mountain vacation. When she was on the trail, she pulled up the hem of her skirt and

*Emilie Klug's unusual appearance and curious habits com-
bined to make her a legend.*

pinned it around her waist, creating a receptacle for carrying a
sleeping bag and other equipment. (Nineteenth century women
who wondered how to cope with long skirts while hiking could
have benefited from Emilie's example.) She also had hooks on her
belt from which she hung a knife, a saucepan, a camera, and various cloth bags filled with chocolate, raisins and other food.

Klug usually began her White Mountain visit with a brief stay
at a hotel in order to gather provisions and prepare for her hikes.
Once she was ready to go, she customarily headed to an ice cave
on the floor of Huntington Ravine on Mount Washington. Here
she stashed some of her provisions before setting out on her wan-

Emilie Klug slept wherever she found herself at night. This photo shows her drying out after a rainstorm.

derings. Although she roamed here and there, she spent most of her time on the Presidential Range. She usually camped out wherever she found herself at night, although she sometimes stayed at a natural rock shelter she had found near the Crawford Path on the cone of Mount Washington.

Because she frequently slept out in the open, rain would occasionally drench Emilie's clothing and equipment. When this happened, she would simply wait for good weather and then lay her wet outer clothing on some rocks, sit down with a book, and wait until the clothes were dry. Milton MacGregor, a hutmaster at the Lakes of the Clouds Hut, wrote an *Appalachia* article about Emilie in which he described coming across her once when she was drying out after a storm. Many of Emilie's belongings were spread out around her, and she was reading a book of poetry, completely at peace with the world. MacGregor spent some time talking with her about her travels. She never complained about the bad weather; instead, she spoke about the flowers that she had seen and the birds that she had heard along the trail. MacGregor wrote, "She carried her own sunshine with her."

Klug frequently stopped for a night or two at one of the AMC huts, and the hutmen came to love her. In fact, MacGregor's article about Emilie was entitled "The Best Friend a Hutman Ever Had." She helped around the hut by doing dishes, darning socks and mending clothes for the crew. If a hutman happened to be sick, she would immediately take charge and nurse him back to health, always staying around until her patient improved.

Klug was extremely nearsighted and apparently wore no glasses. However, she came up with an unusual method for viewing the White Mountain scenery. She carried an old, flimsy camera, which was secured with tape and rubber bands, and a little black book for noting the date, time, and place of every picture she took. When she got home to Brooklyn she would have her film developed and then hold the photos close to her eyes in order to see the places that she had visited during the summer.

MacGregor recalled that one picture Emilie Klug took showed a rather spectral figure floating over Carter Lake near the Carter Notch Hut. A man named Jock Davis had once been a guide in and around Carter Notch, and legend had it that Jock's ghost returned to the Notch on occasion. Emilie insisted that her photograph depicted Jock and absolutely refused to acknowledge that it might be a double xposure.

With Klug's poor eyesight, it is a wonder that she could negotiate the rough and rocky trails of the Presidential Range without mishap. She apparently never had any accidents but she lost her way from time to time. On one occasion, she became confused about her direction, and some hutmen found her wandering around within fifty feet of the Lakes of the Clouds Hut in the morning mist.

When she was out on the trails, the hutmen frequently tried to keep track of her. Once they invited her to a hutmen's party scheduled for a Saturday night at the Pinkham Notch Camp. Beginning early in the week, reports of her whereabouts went from hut to hut. She was seen at Madison Hut on Monday, someplace else on Tuesday. By Saturday, she was sighted at Hermit Lake in the floor of Tuckerman Ravine, and everyone was sure Emilie would make it to the party. But, as usual, she lost her way and arrived at Pinkham Notch on Sunday morning, too late for the festivities.

Klug was hiking in the White Mountains as early as 1912. In August of that year, *Among the Clouds* printed a story about a party of three people who were caught in a thunderstorm and forced to spend the night on Mount Monroe. As the three people huddled under a makeshift shelter, they were surprised to hear a woman's voice. It was Emilie Klug, searching for the summit of Mount Washington. She explained that she had been near the refuge hut (erected in 1901 not far from the place where William Curtis perished) and had decided to continue on to the summit. When the thunderstorm began, Emilie lay flat on the ground and waited until it had passed. By then, darkness was settling over the mountains, and somehow she began heading in the wrong direction and ended up on Mount Monroe. The leader of the party convinced Emilie to remain with them for the night. The article said Klug had been a member of the German and Austrian Alpine Club, and her highest ascent was the Gross Glockner in the Tyrol, a peak about 13,000 feet high.

Emilie Klug returned to Stuttgart, Germany, in the 1930s, supposedly to care for a dying sister. Although she had hoped to return to the United States, she was prevented from leaving Germany when World War II began. However, she continued her AMC membership and tried to keep in touch with old friends.

The Mount Washington Observatory library has a charming letter that Emilie wrote to Stuart and Calista Harris. A biology professor at Boston University, Stuart Harris worked many summers in the AMC huts. Dated January 3, 1947, the letter began as follows: "Dear Friends, The first Christmas greeting since the war ended was dear Calista's letter and it made me almost cry for joy and at the same time homesickness to be so far away from my mountain friends whom I will never see again, as I am too old and ill to return to my adopted country." Emilie asked many questions about old friends and what was happening in the mountains, and she expressed her hope that "all the Hut boys that had to go to war returned safely." After explaining that a stroke had left her partly paralyzed, she concluded the letter with this touching note: "I hope heaven has mountains too. With love to everybody. Your friend, Emilie Klug."

A brief item in a 1961 issue of *Appalachia* announced that Emilie Klug had died, thus ending the story of one of the most endearing characters ever to walk the trails of the White Mountains.

10: Remarkable Feats

THE 1858 EDITION of J. H. Spaulding's *Guide and Historical Relics of the White Mountains* contains the following item under the heading "Remarkable Feats in White-Mountain Life": "The 25th of July, 1855, a lady by the name of Branch walked from the Glen to Tip-Top and back, the same day, on a bet of one thousand dollars. She accomplished the feat, and danced at the Glen in the evening. The cause of the bet was on account of her weight being 230 lbs. She was of medium height, and the heaviest lady that ever visited Tip-Top."

Although the story of Miss or Mrs. Branch's exploit sounds implausible, this much is certain. Many people have attempted to break a record or achieve a significant "first" on Mount Washington or the Presidential Range, and a number of women have been among them. These are the stories of several women who dared to perform remarkable feats on the Great Range.

ELUTHERA CRAWFORD FREEMAN
AND PLACENTIA CRAWFORD DURGIN
The First Women to Climb Mount Washington in Winter

Climbing Mount Washington in the winter is considered a significant mountaineering feat. Although the mountain is not especially high or steep, the arctic conditions near the summit and the possibility of being caught in a sudden, violent storm can make it an extremely dangerous place to be. In fact, the weather is so severe that some modern day mountaineers have used the mountain as a training ground for ascents of Everest and Denali.

A number of winter ascents of Mount Washington were made in the years between 1858 and 1871. The first winter ascent took place in December of 1858 when Lucius Hartshorn, a resident of

Lancaster and deputy sheriff of Coos County, climbed to the summit to attach some property in connection with a legal dispute. Samuel Spaulding, a former owner of the summit houses, and Benjamin Osgood, a well-known guide, accompanied Hartshorn on the climb. Four years later, three men from Lancaster ascended the mountain in February just for the fun of it. Caught by a sudden snowstorm, they had to spend two days and nights in the old Summit House. During the winter of 1870-1871, a scientific team occupied the summit for the first time, and the team members (including J.H. Huntington, after whom Huntington Ravine is named) climbed the mountain many times that season. All of these winter ascents were accomplished by men.

The first women to climb Mount Washington in winter were Eluthera Crawford Freeman and Placentia Crawford Durgin. Both women were daughters of mountain pioneers Lucy and Ethan Allen Crawford. Lucy was one of the first women to climb Mount Washington during the regular season, so it seems appropriate that her daughters were the first to make a winter ascent.

The Crawford daughters completed their historic climb in the latter part of February 1874. In a letter written from Jefferson on February 20, Placentia Durgin said she arrived at the White Mountains in the middle of February and, a few days later, set out by sleigh from Jefferson with her sister; her brother, William Crawford; and her nephew, Ethan Crawford Jr. They rode twenty miles to the base of Mount Washington and, shortly after noon, began climbing on foot up the trestles of the Cog Railway. The men led the way, each man having a strap around his waist that the women held on to for security as they climbed. The foursome stopped often to rest, enjoy the view, and, as Placentia wrote, "occasionally to laugh at the ludicrous appearance we must make." They were exercising vigorously and felt comfortably warm, but as they approached the summit, the wind began to howl and the air was so cold that icicles formed on whiskers and noses and their eyebrows and eyelashes were laced with frost.

Ethan Crawford Jr. rushed ahead to the Signal Station to warn the inhabitants that two ladies were coming. After the winter occupation of the summit in 1870-1871, the U.S. Signal Service, which later became the U.S. Weather Bureau, began maintaining a weather station on Mount Washington. On their arrival at the station, the party learned the wind speed was fifty miles per hour and the temperature eight degrees below zero.

After spending a comfortable night in the warmth of the Signal Station, the Crawford party arose at six and ate a bounteous breakfast. The weather was clear and the view "indescribably grand." As they prepared to leave, the women felt enormous pride to be "the pioneer ladies to the summit of Mount Washington, in winter season." On their descent, the women had to dig their boot heels into the hard, crusty snow to keep from sliding, but with assistance from the men, they arrived at the base of the mountain in about two and one-half hours. Everyone returned safely to Jefferson by five o'clock in the afternoon.

According to White Mountain historian Frederick Kilbourne, twenty-eight years went by before another woman, Dr. Mary Lakeman, successfully climbed Mount Washington in the winter. And one hundred and six years would pass before any women carried out an even more remarkable feat—the winter Presidential traverse.

ANNIE SMITH PECK
The Presidential Traverse

In 1897, Annie Smith Peck, a forty-six-year-old woman who was one of America's foremost mountaineers, spent the summer at the Ravine House in Randolph, New Hampshire. Peck earned her living as a lecturer, and she devoted much of her time to preparing her lectures for the coming season. However, in early September, she took time from her work to accomplish a significant mountaineering feat that began right outside the Ravine House door. Peck went up Mount Madison and continued across the Presidential

Range, climbing nine peaks in one day. This exploit has come to be known as a Presidential traverse.

Peck was not the first person to complete a Presidential traverse. That honor belongs to Eugene B. Cook, the AMC explorer and trail builder, and George Sargent, a fellow member of the Ravine House group. On September 27, 1882, Cook and Sargent left the Ravine House at five in the morning, walked across the ridge of the Presidential Range, stopped for dinner at an inn in Crawford Notch, and then headed back to Randolph via the Cherry Mountain Road. Arriving back at the Ravine House early the next morning, they completed a hike of close to forty-three miles in slightly over twenty hours.

Peck did not travel as far as Cook and Sargent, but she crossed the range entirely alone. In addition, she climbed to the top of Mounts Madison, Adams, Jefferson, Clay, Washington, Monroe, Franklin, Pleasant, and Clinton (Pierce), while Cook and Sargent took a route that skirted some of these summits. Today, the Presidential traverse sometimes includes Mount Jackson and Mount Webster. However, these mountains were not accessible from the Crawford Path at the time of Peck's exploit.

For Annie Peck, challenges such as the Presidential traverse were nothing new; undertakings that others found difficult or dangerous appealed to her. Peck was born in Providence, Rhode Island, to parents who were well-to-do and rather conventional when one considers the unconventional daughter they produced. During her girlhood, Annie was so distressed when her three older brothers refused to allow her to join their games, that she vowed to surpass them at whatever they did. This determination to outdo men remained with her all her life and probably provided the motivation for her many achievements.

Peck earned an undergraduate degree in Greek from the University of Michigan in 1878, went on to acquire a master's degree, and then taught Latin at Purdue University and Smith College. She was one of the first women in the United States to

Annie Smith Peck in the clothes she wore to climb the Matterhorn in 1895. She caused a controversy by wearing pants.

serve as a college professor. Eventually she gave up teaching and supported herself entirely by lecturing. At first, her lectures focused on Greek and Roman archaeology, but after she distinguished herself as a mountaineer, she had a new subject guaranteed to draw crowds. Peck's slender, feminine appearance often surprised audiences. Apparently, people expected a woman mountaineer to be large and muscular.

Peck's interest in mountaineering had been kindled in 1885 when she visited the Swiss Alps and immediately fell in love with mountains. Peck later wrote, "My allegiance previously given to the sea was transferred for all time to the mountains, the Matterhorn securing the first place in my affection." Peck resolved to climb the Matterhorn and immediately began preparing with climbs of lesser peaks. When she set out to do something, Peck was "a monster of persistence," in the words of one of her biographers. In 1895, she achieved her goal, becoming the third woman to reach the Matterhorn's summit. Her climb won her instant celebrity along with considerable notoriety because her climbing outfit consisted of canvas pants, a long tunic and a felt hat. Peck's clothing would seem quite acceptable today, but in 1895, people were shocked by a woman wearing pants.

After her Matterhorn adventure, Peck ascended two major mountains in Mexico: 17,887-foot-high Popocatepetl, the famous volcano, and 18,701-foot-high Mount Orizaba. On Mount Orizaba she set a world altitude record for women. Both climbs took place in 1897, the same year she undertook her easier but still impressive White Mountain adventure.

A description of Peck's Presidential traverse appeared in *The White Mountain Echo* in July of 1898. Reprinted from an interview published in *The New York Sun*, the account emphasized all of the dangers of her hike, making it sound especially dramatic. We learn that at five in the morning on September 3, following a hearty breakfast, Peck left the Ravine House wearing the same costume she had worn on her Matterhorn ascent. She also carried a linen skirt. Peck said she ordinarily would have started her hike by wearing the skirt, but no guests at the Ravine House were up, so she rolled the skirt into a bundle and hung it from her belt. A small bag containing a sandwich, chocolate, raisins, and a small bottle of brandy also hung from her belt.

Although the White Mountains can be dangerously cold in September, especially above tree line, Peck carried no jacket. "I carried no wrap, though I would have been glad to have one," Peck said. "Every ounce of weight counts." She then explained that the skirt weighed about two pounds. For most nineteenth century women, it was unthinkable to appear in public in anything but a skirt. It is surprising that Peck bowed to this custom on her Presidential traverse, especially when one considers that she had been photographed in her Matterhorn outfit. Perhaps the uproar over her pants troubled her.

Peck climbed up the Valley Way, a trail originating near the Ravine House, and reached the summit of Mount Madison in the astonishing time of two hours and twenty minutes—or so she claimed. On her way to the next peak, Mount Adams, she tried a shortcut someone had told her about. It proved a costly mistake both in time and energy, for she lost the trail and was soon floundering among large rocks and thick scrub. Aware that lives had been lost on the Presidential Range, Peck was sure she was in the same place where a violinist from the Summit House had disappeared several years earlier. "I thought of him and hoped I wouldn't run across his remains," Peck said. She finally arrived at Mount Adams' summit after a climb she described as harder than the Matterhorn.

Peck crossed over the summits of Mounts Jefferson and Clay, followed the trail until she reached the Cog Railway, and then walked up the tracks to Mount Washington's summit. When she reached the Summit House, she immediately put on her skirt. It was almost one o'clock, and Peck was worried about the time. It would be dark early, and she had to go through some thick woods at the end of the Crawford Path. Nevertheless, she rested, ate heartily, and rested some more, remaining on the summit for almost two hours. When she resumed her hike, she waited until she was a suitable distance from the Summit House; then she took off her skirt, rolled it up, and once again hung it from her belt.

Peck continued across the range, climbing Mounts Monroe, Franklin, Pleasant, and Clinton (Pierce). After she passed over the latter peak, her ninth, she was elated as she realized her traverse was almost over. With darkness closing in, she negotiated a rough trail through the woods and reached the Crawford House shortly after seven o'clock. Peck summed up her achievement by saying, "There are not many men who would be up to the trip, and no other woman has done it."

Was Annie Smith Peck the first woman to traverse the entire Presidential Range? Probably not. An 1889 article in *The White Mountain Echo* reported that Miss M.A. Knowles had "covered all the Presidential peaks in one day, a feat that would stagger most men." Martha A. Knowles was an AMC member and a frequent trail companion of Martha F. Whitman. Knowles left no description of her Presidential traverse, and by 1897, her feat must have been forgotten. As a result, Annie Peck, who was skilled at self-promotion, grabbed credit for it.

After her Presidential traverse, Peck continued her adventurous ways. Hoping to "conquer a virgin peak, to attain some height where no man had previously stood," she set her sights on Mount Huascaran in Peru and in 1908, after six attempts, finally succeeded in reaching its summit. She was just shy of age fifty-eight at the time. In 1911, she made a first ascent of Peru's Mount Coropuna and planted a "Votes for Women" banner on the summit.

Age never slowed down Annie Peck. She wrote books, traveled, and climbed mountains to the end of her life. For her last mountain climb, she returned to the White Mountains and, at age eighty-two, climbed Mount Madison. Two years later, on July 18, 1935, she passed away.

LAURA WATERMAN, NATALIE DAVIS, AND DEBBIE O'NEILL
The First Women to Complete a Winter Presidential Traverse

In February of 1980, three women—Natalie Davis, Debbie O'Neill, and Laura Waterman—set out to walk across the Presidential Range in winter. All three were experienced winter hikers who had worked as instructors in the AMC Winter Mountaineering School. At the time of their exploit, Natalie was a high school English teacher, Debbie was a physical therapist, and Laura was a homesteader and writer. A year earlier, Laura and her husband Guy Waterman had co-authored *Backwoods Ethics*, and they were just beginning research on *Forest and Crag*, a book about the history of Northeastern hiking.

The winter Presidential traverse can be a formidable task; it involves extensive hiking above tree line in weather that is often

Laura Waterman on Cannon Mountain.

characterized by sub-zero temperatures and savage winds. Herschel Parker and Ralph Larrabee, two proficient AMC climbers, completed the first winter traverse in December of 1896. Since that time, parties of men had done the traverse, but as far as Davis, O'Neill, and Waterman knew, no team of women had ever attempted it.

Laura Waterman described their adventure in an article published in the book *Leading Out*. She began by explaining that the winter Presidential traverse is considered to be the mark of an expert New England winter mountaineer, yet success in carrying it out depends more on the weather than anything else. If the weather is bad, the traverse is virtually impossible. If the weather is good, the traverse can be rather easy to complete. "It's a waltz—like walking along a slightly bumpy sidewalk," Waterman stated.

The women decided to follow the usual route for a Presidential traverse. They would take the Valley Way to the col (a low point or saddle) between Mounts Madison and Adams and, after climbing those peaks, continue across the rest of the Presidential Range. They elected to cross over all the summits instead of taking the trail that goes around them. As Waterman wrote, "We wanted to do the real thing. Going over the summits would make it harder, but it's also what the traverse is all about."

On their first day, Waterman, Davis and O'Neill hiked up the Valley Way and set up camp in the woods below the Madison col. Leaving their packs in the tent, they climbed Mount Madison that afternoon. Their only problem was a severe wind that kept them on all fours on the descent.

The next day, the weather was ideal—sunny and warm with no wind. The women strolled across the summits of Mounts Adams, Jefferson, Clay and Washington, arriving at the Lakes of the Clouds Hut late in the afternoon. They dropped their packs in a basement room left open for winter backpackers and literally ran up nearby Mount Monroe. At this point, Waterman, Davis and O'Neill were pleased with their progress, but they were also

Natalie Davis (left), and Laura Waterman (right) on a winter hike.

worrying that their traverse would be "too easy." As Waterman wrote, "We wanted to find out how we would manage in bad weather, too. That was one reason why we were out here."

Before they fell asleep that night the wind began to roar "like an angry lion" and they knew that they would have a chance to prove themselves. When they set out the next morning, the wind was so powerful that it knocked down both Waterman and Davis as they were walking on the path around Mount Monroe. Realizing that they would have great difficulty completing the traverse in such brutal weather, they turned around and were dejectedly heading back to the hut for another night. And then the wind abated slightly. "Our footsteps slowed as we felt the wind lessen," Waterman remembered. O'Neill turned to Davis and asked her if she wanted to continue, and Natalie Davis answered with an emphatic "Yes!"

The three women immediately changed direction and headed back into the wind. They managed to make it over Mounts Franklin and Eisenhower without much difficulty. The wind strengthened as they approached Mount Clinton (Pierce), but they left their packs at the base and scrambled to the summit. They had made it! Thrilled that they had just become the first party of women to complete a winter Presidential traverse, they "shook hands, jumping up and down, hugging and thumping each other on the back." And thanks to the strong wind, it had not been a "waltz." As Laura Waterman later wrote, "It was a good last day; we'd had to work for it."

FLORENCE MURRAY CLARK
The First Woman to Drive a Dog Team to Mount Washington's Summit

On March 30, 1926, Arthur Walden drove a team of sled dogs, led by the famous Chinook, up a snow-packed Auto Road to the summit of Mount Washington. It was a hazardous undertaking, for the route included some steep, icy sections that were extremely difficult for the dogs to cross. Seven men, including two newsreel photographers who filmed the adventure, accompanied Walden. The feat was unprecedented, and no one expected it to be repeated—at least not anytime soon. Yet, a mere six years later, on April 3-4, 1932, Florence Murray Clark, a young woman from North Woodstock, New Hampshire, drove a dog team to the summit entirely alone.

Florence Murray Clark and her dogs after making the first solo ascent of Mount Washington by dog sled. Photograph by Robert Monahan.

At the time of her adventure, Clark had never even climbed Mount Washington. However, this lively, attractive woman was an experienced sled dog driver with a reputation for courage and determination. If anyone had the grit to drive a team to Mount Washington's summit, it was Florence.

Born and raised in New York City, Florence Murray acquired an interest in dogs when a neighbor named Edward Clark brought home a team of sled dogs from Labrador. Florence and Ed Clark were married in 1922, and they moved to West Milan, New Hampshire, to raise dogs and establish a raw fur business. By 1928, the Clarks had relocated to North Woodstock where they established Ed Clark's Eskimo Sled Dog Ranch. Florence had a full schedule by this time. In addition to helping her husband on the ranch, she had two sons to care for, and she logged about two thousand miles each winter training her dogs for races.

F. Allen Burt interviewed Florence Clark about her exploit and reported on it in his book, *The Story of Mount Washington*. He learned that the idea of driving a team to Mount Washington's summit was suggested to Florence by John Brady of *The Boston Post*. At first, she had no interest in the proposal, but something—perhaps recognition of the publicity value of the climb—caused her to change her mind.

Clark's first two attempts to reach the summit failed. On January 13, 1932, with a team of eight dogs and accompanied by five men, Florence almost reached the summit but turned back when one of the men lost consciousness. He was probably in the early stages of hypothermia for the weather was cold, wet, and windy. The next attempt began on February 21st. Clark and three men, including the photographer Winston Pote, started at ten o'clock at night, hoping to arrive at the summit on the two hundredth anniversary of George Washington's birth. This time the party was thwarted by a frost storm and a dogfight. To add to their problems, Pote was lost for a brief time. With all of these troubles, they elected to go back down the mountain.

On her third try, Florence Clark planned to take two men along, but due to a confusion about dates, the men could not come. Determined to make the trip alone, she started out on April 3 with five dogs and a sled loaded down with about one hundred and fifty pounds of gear. Her goal that day was the Halfway House, a refuge located about four miles up the Auto Road. She arrived there safely around seven in the evening and after cleaning out snow and debris left by an earlier occupant, spent the night.

Winston Pote had told Clark that a trunk in the Halfway House held some crampons she could borrow for her trip. But when she opened the trunk the next morning, the crampons were missing. Her rubber boots were totally inadequate for what lay ahead, yet Clark decided to continue. All went well until the team reached the five-mile mark on the Auto Road. At this point, a huge drift covered the road for approximately three-quarters of a mile. The dogs headed up the drift, which grew steeper and steeper. Suddenly the sled struck ice, turned on its side and began sliding toward the edge of a steep incline. If the sled went over the edge, it would plunge thousands of feet to jagged rocks below, taking the dogs with it.

Vaulting over the sled, Clark struggled to hold it from below with her shoulder. Somehow, she managed to reach an axe strapped to the sled, cut a wedge in the ice, and ram the axe handle into the opening to hold the sled. She chopped a second wedge with another axe. Then she unlashed and moved the heavy load on the sled, allowing the dogs to pull the sled to a safer spot.

Unfortunately, she placed a duffle bag on a rock, and as the dogs moved past, one of the young ones playfully sniffed at it, sending it over the edge of the incline. Florence watched with horror as the duffle bag tumbled down about a thousand feet. The duffle contained her sleeping bag, a camera, food, and a valuable gun belonging to her husband. Unwilling to continue without these items, she chained the lead dog and rested briefly to gather her strength. Then she sat down on the snow, and braking with the axe, she slid down and retrieved the bag. The relatively easy descent took her just a few minutes, but the climb back up to the Auto Road took over an hour. Clark had to use her axe both to cut steps and to pull herself up, all the while dragging the duffle bag with her free hand.

Clark finally got her team going again, and the dogs successfully negotiated a tricky section of ice near Chandler Ridge. As the team drew close to the summit, Clark was surprised to see a man and a large dog. She had not expected any reception but discovered that Robert Monahan, who was involved at the time in re-opening the Mount Washington Observatory, had come to the summit that day to check on some details in connection with two accidental deaths. Many years later, Monahan described the encounter in *New Hampshire Profiles*:

> In mid-afternoon…I was surprised to notice a five-dog team approaching the very last pitch on the Carriage Road. Their driver, the late Florence Clark and a personal friend

for many years, was equally surprised as she approached, unaided, her goal after two heart-breaking failures. Florence said something like, "Leave me alone, Bob, until I make this last stretch to the top. And then I don't know what I can do. Glad you're up today!"

Clark drove the dogs to the summit and posed for a photograph, proud that she had successfully achieved her goal. She was exhausted and wanted only to rest for the night at Camden Cottage, a refuge on the summit. But Monahan told her that a storm had been forecast and suggested that they both get off the mountain before nightfall. So, after a short break, Florence Clark curled up in the sled, and Monahan drove the team down the mountain. "Fortunately, Florence's husband Ed had rigged the sled with a rugged brake, which I stood on for about every minute of the trip," Monahan remembered. The trip down took five hours.

Sadly, Florence Clark's achievement was won at the price of her health. Weakened by her ordeal, she contracted pneumonia and eventually tuberculosis. Although she had some periods of relatively good health when she was able to race her dogs, she never fully recovered and died in 1950.

11: Saving the Land

THE WHITE MOUNTAINS have changed dramatically since the days when Lucy and Ethan Allen Crawford ran their inn in Crawford Notch. Today, high-speed highways bring many visitors to the region—seven million a year, according to one estimate. Instead of the plain and rustic inns operated by the Crawfords, tourists have a wide range of accommodations to choose from—everything from campgrounds to motels to luxury hotels. And the many distractions—the incredible busy-ness of some parts of the mountain region—would have been beyond Lucy and Ethan's comprehension.

In *The White Hills*, Thomas Starr King complained about the people who hurried through the White Mountains in an effort to "do the notches," a popular nineteenth century activity that involved traveling around by stage coach to see the sights in Crawford Notch, Franconia Notch and Pinkham Notch. "A large proportion of the summer travellers in New Hampshire bolt the scenery, as a man, driven by work, bolts his dinner at a restaurant," King wrote. He would have been appalled by some of today's visitors. They race through the mountains in their automobiles, taking little time to appreciate the scenic beauty around them. A few do not come with mountains in mind at all. They are attracted by the amusement parks or the outlet stores or the many other man-made attractions.

Yet, many people still love the mountains and seek them out as a retreat from an increasingly commercial world. It is fortunate that dedicated women have helped protect hundreds of thousands of acres in the White Mountains as state parks and national forest. This allows people to get out of their cars and into the hills, which have become one of the few places left where one can find wilderness or at least something close to it. An earlier chapter described Kate Sleeper Walden's efforts to have a special tract of woodland included in the White Mountain National Forest. Approximately seventy-five years later, two land-conscious women saved a small mountain range as a nature preserve. One of the women was Katharine Fowler-Billings. She left a lasting legacy through her work to protect open space in the White Mountains, and she increased our knowledge of White Mountain geology. The other was Anna Stearns, a philanthropist who used her personal wealth to help others and to protect the environment.

KATHARINE FOWLER-BILLINGS AND ANNA STEARNS

Katharine Fowler was born in 1902 in Little Boar's Head, New Hampshire, a coastal village where her family had a summer home. For the rest of the year, the family lived in Boston. As a young girl Katharine suffered from hay fever, and every summer she huddled miserably on the beach, sneezing and wheezing, while other children romped in the ocean. A doctor suggested she might find relief in the White Mountains, which had a reputation as a haven for hay fever sufferers, so from age seven until her college years, she spent the month of August with a kindly, middle-aged widow who had a home in Randolph, New Hampshire.

These vacations in the White Mountains relieved Katharine's hay fever and brought other benefits as well. She learned to love the mountains and developed a lasting interest in climbing. More importantly, she discovered her life's work. As a young girl, exploring the streams and woods around Randolph, Katharine began wondering about her surroundings: Why were mountains there? What caused the rocks to form? And why was the mountain region so different from the coast? "I vowed that someday I would study geology and answer these questions," she recalled. She kept her promise to herself, graduating from Bryn Mawr with a degree in geology and biology in 1925, earning a master's degree in geology from the University of Wisconsin a year later, and four years after that, acquiring a Ph.D. in geology from Columbia University.

After getting her doctorate, Kay (as she was known to her friends) traveled the world and spent several adventure-filled years prospecting for gold and other minerals in Sierra Leone. Returning to the United States in the mid 1930s, she took a job teaching geology at Wellesley College. During the summer, she worked in the field, mapping the region around Mount Cardigan in central New Hampshire.

Through her summer work, Kay met and fell in love with Marland Billings, a young Harvard geology professor who was making a name for himself with his outstanding geological work in New England. When Billings proposed marriage, Kay agonized over whether to accept, for she treasured her independence and wondered if she could successfully combine marriage with a career. She finally agreed, and in 1938, Katharine and Marland Billings were married. They settled in Wellesley, and Kay resigned her teaching job to take care of a son, born in 1939, and a daughter, adopted the next year.

In the 1940s and 1950s, Kay Fowler-Billings was a woman ahead of her time, one of the few who successfully combined family with a career. Although she devoted most of her time to her children, she found a way to continue working in geology. She conducted research a few hours a day, taught some courses at Tufts University, and served as geology curator of the National Historical Museum in Boston. In the summer, she headed for the White Mountains to work in the field with her husband.

In addition to his teaching responsibilities, Marland Billings had taken on an ambitious project: producing a geological map of New Hampshire. He had divided the state into blocks or quadrangles, and he and his graduate students set to work mapping them. Immediately after their marriage, the Billings began mapping the Mount Washington region together.

Other geologists who worked in the White Mountains found the dense vegetation on the mountainsides a barrier to their work. Marland Billings had a solution to this problem. He and Kay climbed the streambeds where the bedrock was already exposed. After thoroughly investigating all the streams, they explored the ridges between the streams and studied the outcroppings and exposed rock on the higher slopes.

For mapping the Mount Washington area, the Billings followed every stream on the Presidential Range. This strenuous work involved a lot of bushwhacking and constant battles with black flies and mosquitoes, but the results were worth it. The Billings' detailed observations and careful analysis of what they found has given the scientific community a much better understanding of the complex structural geology of the White Mountains. In 1946, they published the fruit of their efforts, *Geology of the Mount Washington quadrangle, New Hampshire*. Next, the Billings mapped the Gorham Quadrangle, and this culminated in the publication of *Geology of the Gorham quadrangle, New Hampshire —Maine* in 1975.

By the 1960s, the Billings were beginning to think about retirement and decided to build a home in Bartlett, New Hampshire, a town along the Saco River to the south of Crawford Notch. Their small house had "a glorious view of Mount Washington," and it offered easy access to activities they enjoyed: hiking in the summer and snowshoeing and skiing in the winter.

Over the years, conservation had become a vital concern for Kay, and she had participated in some environmental causes during her years in Wellesley. After moving to Bartlett, she again found herself acting as "nature's watchdog," a term she used to describe herself in her autobiography, *Stepping-Stones*. Her involvement came about quite unexpectedly. One morning, the Billings were awakened by the clamor of a plane flying over their house at a low altitude. Kay ran outdoors to see what was happening and saw a tow-plane pulling a glider. Almost overnight, a gliderport had sprouted across the river from their home. "It was the beginning of a nightmare," she later wrote. "The noise of the tow-planes made life miserable for all who lived in the formerly peaceful valley."

The Billings got together with other concerned citizens to hire a lawyer to fight this intrusion. The legal battle dragged on for two years, during which time the gliderport continued to expand. Finally, just before the case was due to be argued in court, the owner offered to sell the gliderport. The price was excessive, but Kay managed to obtain a bank loan and raise other funds through private donations, and the offer was accepted. Her next problem was what to do with the land—sixty-two acres of floodplain. The town of Bartlett had no interest in purchasing it, and she refused to sell to developers. Eventually someone who wanted to establish a family campground offered to buy the property, and the sale was made with certain restrictions to be sure that the campground would be properly maintained. Although the property sold for half of what had been paid for it, Kay Fowler-Billings felt "glad to take our losses" so the land would be saved as open space.

The gliderport problem was solved quickly compared to the next cause Kay championed. As she grew older and could no longer "master the rugged higher peaks of the Presidentials," she found pleasure in climbing the Green Hills, a small mountain range to the east of North Conway. Extending south from Mount Kearsarge North, the Green Hills include Hurricane Mountain, Black Cap, Peaked Mountain, Middle Mountain, Cranmore Mountain, and Rattlesnake Mountain. Hikers who reach the summits of some of these hills are rewarded with lovely views of Mount Washington and the Presidential Range. The Green Hills appeared to be a prime candidate for development. Kay abhorred the idea of vacation homes marching up the lovely hillsides, and she resolved to save these mountains so others could continue to enjoy them.

At first, she focused on Peaked Mountain. She had explored this mountain thoroughly and was convinced that the north side had never been logged for it contained mature hemlocks and pines as well as many beautiful endangered plants. She also cherished

Katharine Fowler-Billings on the summit of Peaked Mountain.

the mountain because its bare, glacier-scoured slopes offered "outstanding textbook examples of earth processes."

Beginning in the late 1960s, Kay Fowler-Billings worked for more than two decades to permanently protect Peaked Mountain. A granite company owned all the land in the Green Hills, and as a first step, she approached the owners, hoping to persuade them to sell the mountain, or, better yet, donate it to a charitable organization. But the owners refused to do either.

Hiking on the Gulfside Trail near the summit of Mount Washington. Anna Stearns (far left) was 83 at the time. Kay Billings (second from left) was 76.

After this rejection, she tried to build strong support for the idea of protecting the mountain. She climbed Peaked Mountain frequently and kept a growing list of the flowers and plants that she found there, hoping to establish the mountain's value as a natural area. She also took many friends to the mountain to interest them in its preservation.

One of these friends was Anna Stearns, an active member of the AMC and the Randolph Mountain Club. Like Kay Billings, Anna Stearns had learned to love the White Mountains during her childhood, when her parents brought her to the region on a vacation. Anna Stearns graduated from Vassar, and then, after obtaining a master's degree in landscape architecture, she traveled the world, visiting and studying gardens. Although she loved to travel, the White Mountains were a constant in her life and she eventually settled in Randolph, where her parents had built a summer home. Stearns shared Kay Billings' interest in hiking, and the two women had climbed all the peaks of the Presidential Range together, making some of these climbs when Anna Stearns was in her early eighties and Kay was well into her seventies. When Kay took Anna to Peaked Mountain, she gained a strong ally. As Billings later wrote, "At every opportunity, . . . Anna drove down from Randolph and we set off for the ledges of Peaked Mountain, bushwhacking in all directions and adding to our growing list of flora."

In the early 1980s, Fowler-Billings presented her case for saving Peaked Mountain to the Nature Conservancy, one of the nation's premier land-saving organizations. The Conservancy agreed that the land should be protected and began talking to the granite company. By this time, the company's owners were willing to sell, but their price was much too high.

More years passed, and Kay Fowler-Billings kept searching for some way to save Peaked Mountain. Then, suddenly, in the late 1980s, the granite company sold all of the Green Hills to a local developer. The Nature Conservancy immediately began negotiating with the developer and learned he was willing to sell 2,800 acres—almost all the high land (only Hurricane Mountain was excluded)— at a reasonable price. The only problem was raising the necessary funds. Although The Nature Conservancy was willing to loan money to make the purchase, the loan would have to be repaid.

Fowler-Billings described what happened next in her autobiography:

> I had an urgent call from Boston asking me to talk to my friends to see what funds might be available. I hate to ask my friends for money. Hesitating, I approached…Anna Stearns, who had hiked so many times with me in these beautiful hills…. To my utter amazement, she said she would buy the whole of the Green Hills as a long-hoped-for memorial to her parents. The Green Hills were saved. Now they would be green forever.

Anna Stearns was the only child and sole heir of Harold Stearns, the founder of the Estabrook fountain pen company. This generous woman spent her life using her personal wealth to help others. Over the years, she gave many scholarships to young people who needed help to go to college, and in the 1960s, she established the Anna Stearns Foundation to make grants to help women, children, and the environment. She had always been devoted to her parents, and for a long time, she had wanted to thank them for introducing her to the White Mountains by preserving some special land in their memory. With the purchase of the Green Hills, she realized her dream.

Anna Stearns was elderly and in poor health when Kay spoke with her about saving the Green Hills. She died at age ninety-four in April of 1990, shortly before the purchase was completed. However, Stearns did live long enough to know that an agreement to buy the land had been signed. Anna Stearns' legacy to the White Mountains continues. In 2000, the Anna Stearns Foundation provided a grant to help purchase the forests surrounding the Pond of Safety, a historic pond in the hills behind Randolph.

The 2,800-acre Green Hills Preserve was dedicated at a celebration in North Conway in the summer of 1991. A year later, Katharine Fowler-Billings published an article in *Appalachia* about saving this land, and she was modest about her own contribution, giving most of the credit to Anna Stearns. She also arranged to have an inscription honoring Stearns carved into a granite slab on the top of Black Cap Mountain. Stearns played an indispensable role. She had shared Katharine Fowler-Billings' interest in the Green Hills and had provided the funds to buy the land. However, Fowler-Billings deserves to be remembered as the moving force behind the Green Hills Preserve.

Summing up the importance of the preserve, Katharine Fowler-Billings wrote, "It is a place to escape from the pressures of life in a busy, demanding world, an island of refuge, where one can still enjoy peace and solitude. Its value as a natural area will be its greatest appeal in the future when so few such places will be left."

Katharine Fowler-Billings died in 1997. Her life and involvement with the White Mountains had spanned virtually the entire twentieth century. Like the many other women who have been the subject of this book, she enriched us all with her enduring love for the White Mountains.

Appendix

UNFORTUNATELY, I was unable to include a chapter for all of the women I discovered in my research. Some were omitted because it was difficult to document their relationship with the mountains. Other women may have played a role in White Mountain life, but they were not prominent players on its stage. And in some cases, women were not included because their stories simply did not fit easily into the narrative. Following are brief descriptions of a few women who deserve mention:

WEETAMOO

With the possible exception of Nancy (see Chapter One), no other woman has as many White Mountain sites named for her as Weetamoo, a female chief of the Pocassets. The sites include lovely Weetamoo Falls in the Great Gulf, Mount Weetamoo in Campton, and the Weetamoo Trail on Mount Chocorua. Anyone hiking the Weetamoo Trail will go through Weetamoo Glen and pass by Weetamoo Rock. The Six Husbands Trail in the Great Gulf also has a connection with Weetamoo, for, according to tradition, she was married six times.

Despite the prevalence of her name in White Mountain geography, it is uncertain if Weetamoo ever visited the region. The territory of the Pocasset tribe was in southwestern Massachusetts and Rhode Island—quite a long distance from the White Mountains. John Greenleaf Whittier is probably responsible for all the attention given to Weetamoo. He incorrectly identified her as Passaconaway's daughter in "The Bridal of Pennacook," a poem with a White Mountains setting.

The real Weetamoo lived from about 1635 to 1676, and her name appears in histories about King Philip's War. Although

Weetamoo had several husbands, no evidence indicates that she had as many as six.

MARGARET (OR JESSIE) GUERNSEY

Margaret Guernsey is credited with discovering the Flume in Franconia Notch sometime in the early 1800s. As the story goes, Mrs. Guernsey was elderly and perhaps a bit senile. She liked to fish and often wandered off into the woods, looking for a good place to drop a fishing line. One day, she told her family about a beautiful cascade that she had found. No one paid much attention, but she mentioned the spot so often that people finally began to take her seriously. Someone went to the site with Mrs. Guernsey and found what is known today as the Flume. As people heard about the Flume, it gradually attracted many tourists. Some versions of the story identify the discoverer of the Flume as Jessie Guernsey, the wife of David Guernsey, a pioneer settler in the Franconia region.

MRS. DANIEL PATCH

Mrs. Daniel Patch was the first woman to climb Mount Moosilauke, according to William Little, author of a history of Warren, New Hampshire, a town near the base of the mountain. Little wrote that Mrs. Patch "brought her tea-pot with her, and made herself a good cup of tea over a fire kindled from the hackmatacks, bleached white, so many of which you see standing like skeletons down on the shoulders of the mountain...." He failed to give Mrs. Patch's first name or the date of her ascent. The first trail up Moosilauke was cut in 1840. Presumably, Mrs. Patch used a trail to get up the mountain, so her climb would have taken place sometime after that date.

EMILY SELINGER

During the latter half of the nineteenth century, many of the grand hotels had artists-in-residence. Typically, the artists would paint in a studio located on the hotel grounds. Frequently, the artists painted local scenes and landscapes, producing "tourist art" that people could purchase as a souvenir of their visit.

Emily Selinger (1848-1927) and her husband Jean Paul Selinger had a summer art studio at the Glen House from the early 1880s until 1894. When the Glen House burned in 1894, the Selingers were fortunate in being able to take over Frank Shapleigh's studio at the Crawford House. Emily Selinger specialized in flower paintings and Venetian watercolors, while Jean Paul painted local subjects and portraits. Emily and Paul Selinger were excellent conversationalists and played an important part in the hotel's social life. When not summering in the White Mountains, the Selingers were active in Boston art circles. They continued as summer artists-in-residence at the Crawford House until Jean Paul Selinger died in 1909.

ANNE WHITNEY

Anne Whitney (1821-1915) was a poet and sculptor who produced such significant works as the marble statue of Samuel Adams in the U.S. Capitol, and a seated figure of Charles Sumner near Harvard Square in Cambridge. In 1882, Whitney bought a farm in Shelburne, New Hampshire, and began spending her summers in the White Mountains. She developed an interest in nature and conservation and joined the AMC in 1894. Three years later, she bought twelve acres of land around the Leadmine Bridge on the Androscoggin River in Shelburne, the location Thomas Starr King had praised as the perfect viewing point for Mount Madison. After removing some ramshackle buildings from the property, Whitney gave it to the AMC. A few years later, she gave an additional twenty-five acres on the northern side of the river. Unfortunately, the Berlin Electric Light Company built a dam and a power plant on nearby land, destroying the perfect view of Mount Madison that Starr King had praised. In 1935, the AMC gave the land to the State of New Hampshire, and today it is part of the

Leadmine State Forest. A year after Whitney made her initial gift of land to the AMC, her friend Sarah Fay of Boston gave the club approximately 200 acres of land in North Woodstock and Lincoln as a memorial to her father. Today the Joseph Story Fay Reservation is also owned by the State of New Hampshire.

ELLEN McROBERTS MASON

The wife of a North Conway innkeeper, Ellen McRoberts Mason wrote poetry, sketches and articles for such publications as *The Granite Monthly, The White Mountain Echo, Among the Clouds, The Portland Transcript,* and *The Boston Herald.* During the period when the timber industry was destroying thousands of acres of land in the White Mountains, Mason took up the cause of forest preservation. She not only wrote about this subject, but in 1901, she joined with eight men to found the Society for the Protection of New Hampshire Forests (SPNHF). Along with the AMC, the SPNHF led the fight to establish national forests in the Eastern part of the United States. Because of the important role Mason played in founding the SPNHF, she was given the honor of naming the group. As chairman of the Forestry Committee of the New Hampshire Federation of Women's Clubs from 1897 to 1905, Mason persuaded the women's clubs to join the SPNHF. The women's clubs provided vital help to the SPNHF as it campaigned for passage of the Weeks Act and for the preservation of Crawford Notch as a state park.

RUTH COLBATH

Ruth Colbath and her husband Thomas lived in a small frame house in Passaconaway, which had been built in 1831 by Thomas Russell, Ruth's grandfather. One day in 1891, Thomas Colbath went out for a walk and never came home. That same night, Ruth Colbath put a light in the window, so her husband could find his way back to the house.

Years passed, and no one knew anything about Thomas

Colbath's whereabouts, yet every night Ruth put her lamp in the window. She continued to do this for an astonishing thirty-nine years! As summer visitors to the mountains heard the story of her vigil, Ruth Colbath acquired legendary status. In November of 1930, she died at the age of eighty. Three years later, to everyone's surprise, Thomas Colbath reappeared at his old home and gave a brief account of his travels. After leaving his wife, he had remained in the Passaconaway region for a year. Then, he had wandered westward and spent some time in California, Cuba, and other places. He never explained why he left or what prompted him to return home.

Today the Russell Colbath House is in the National Register of Historic Places. It is part of the Passaconaway Historic Site, which is located on the north side of the Kancamagus Highway about fourteen miles from the Saco Ranger Station in Conway.

HATTIE EVANS

In 1903, Hattie and Loring Evans came to live in a house perched high on the side of Mount Willard in Crawford Notch. An employee of the Maine Central Railroad, Loring Evans was foreman of a crew responsible for maintaining the section of track that ran through the Notch. Their house, which was known as a "section house," was less than twenty feet away from the tracks. The crew of four men lived in the house with the Evans, and Hattie cooked meals for them and did their laundry.

Although the Evans had been childless when they moved to the section house, four children were born to them during their first eight years in the Notch. Hattie and Loring Evans were thrilled to be blessed with a family, but then tragedy struck. In 1913, a freight engine hit and killed Loring Evans while he was digging out the tracks in a snowstorm. Refusing help from the railroad company, Hattie Evans stayed on in the Notch and continued to run the section house. This brave woman raised her children and provided lodging and meals for the crew until the early 1940s.

For years, people driving through Crawford Notch gazed with wonder at the house, which seemed to cling precariously to the mountainside. The house was finally demolished in 1972. The story of the Evans family and their life in the section house is told in *Life by the Tracks* by Virginia Downs.

FLORENCE MOREY

A twentieth century innkeeper whom many people remember fondly was Florence Morey. She ran the Inn Unique in Hart's Location, at the southern end of Crawford Notch, from about 1920 until her death in 1978 at age ninety-one. The inn was originally a stone manor house, built near Abel Crawford's Mount Crawford House in 1840 by Samuel Bemis, a Boston dentist. Bemis owned considerable acreage in Crawford Notch. When he died, he left his house and all of his property to his long-time estate manager, George W. Morey.

Morey's son Charles married Florence Pendergast, a native of Boston, and brought her to the Notch in 1906. Fourteen years later, Charles and Florence Morey decided to open their home as an inn. Initially, it was known as The Bemis House; but after a few years, the Moreys changed the name to the Notchland Inn. At some point, Florence and her husband had a falling-out, and they parted ways. She ended up with the stone house, which she continued to run as a hotel. In the 1940s, she again changed its name to the Inn Unique. She turned one room into an unusual museum devoted to Dr. Bemis and the Crawford family. An important figure in North Country politics, Florence Morey was the first woman to represent Hart's Location in the New Hampshire legislature.

WOMEN FIRE LOOKOUTS

During World War II, the U.S. Forest Service and some state forestry departments hired women as fire lookouts. It was a hard, lonely job but one with special pleasures for women interested in the natural world. In 1943, Elizabeth Sampson, an executive in the Girl Scouts, "felt the need of getting outdoors—and staying out—as much as possible," as she explained in an *Appalachia* article. When she learned the Forest Service was hiring women as fire lookouts in the White Mountains, she applied for the job and was accepted. That spring, after attending Lookout Training School, Sampson was assigned to the Middle Sister Tower on Mount Chocorua . She lived alone at the fire tower, working fourteen-hour days. In addition to her fire lookout duties, Sampson spotted planes, and when the fire danger was low, she cleared trails. Three other women served as lookouts during the 1943 season. Mrs. Maude S. Bickford was assigned to the fire tower on Black Mountain; Mrs. Barbara B. Mortensen worked on Pine Mountain, and Miss Dorothy Martin manned the fire tower on Kearsarge North.

ELLEN CRAWFORD TEAGUE

Ellen Teague grew up in Philadelphia and came to the White Mountains in 1942 when she married Arthur Teague, the manager of the Cog Railway. While raising six children, she helped her husband manage the railroad. In 1962, the Teagues purchased the Cog Railway. When Arthur died five years later, Ellen became the only woman in the United States who was in charge of running a railroad. She continued to manage the Cog Railway until 1981 when she sold it to a group of investors. Ellen Teague was not related to the Crawfords of Crawford Notch, but she liked to think her maiden name had something to do with her destiny. Teague told the story of her life and her experience running the Cog Railway in the book *I Conquered My Mountain*.

Selected Bibliography

BOOKS

Beals Jr., Edward. *Passaconaway in the White Mountains*. Boston: Richard G. Badger, 1916.

Belcher, C. Francis. *Logging Railroads of the White Mountains*. Boston: The Appalachian Mountain Club, 1980.

Birkett, Bill, and Bill Peascod. *Women Climbing: 200 Years of Achievement*. Seattle: The Mountaineers, 1990.

Burt, F. Allen. *The Story of Mount Washington*. Hanover, New Hampshire: Dartmouth Publications, 1960.

Crawford, Lucy. *History of the White Mountains*. Edited by John Mudge. Etna, New Hampshire: The Durand Press, 1999.

Cross, George N. *Dolly Copp and the Pioneers of the Glen*. Baltimore, Md.: Press of Day Printing Co., 1927.

Cross, George N. *Randolph Old and New*. Town of Randolph, N.H., 1924.

Da Silva, Rachel, ed. *Leading Out: Women Climbers Reaching for the Top*. Seattle: Seal Press, 1992.

Drake, Samuel. *The Heart of the White Mountains*. New York: Harper & Brothers, 1881.

Fowler-Billings, Katharine. *Stepping-Stones: The Reminiscences of a Woman Geologist in the Twentieth Century*. New Haven, Connecticut: The Connecticut Academy of Arts and Sciences, 1996.

Harkness, Marjory Gane. *The Tamworth Narrative*. Freeport, Me.: The Bond Wheelright Co., 1958.

Hawthorne, Nathaniel. *Mosses from an Old Manse, vol. 2*. Boston and New York: Houghton Mifflin Co., 1900.

Hidden, Mabel and Ulitz, Jean, eds. *Tamworth Recollections*. North Conway, N.H.: North Conway Publishing, 1976.

Horne, Ruth B.D. *Conway Through the Years and Whither*. Conway, New Hampshire: Conway Historical Society, 1963.

Kilbourne, Frederick. *Chronicles of the White Mountains*. Boston and New York: Houghton Mifflin Company, 1916.

King, Thomas Starr. *The White Hills: Their Legends, Landscape and Poetry*. Boston: Estes and Lauriat, 1887 reprint of 1859 edition.

Marchalonis, Shirley. *The Worlds of Lucy Larcom*. Athens, Ga.: The University of Georgia Press, 1989.

Martineau, Harriet. *Retrospect of Western Travel*. New York: Saunders & Otley, 1837.

Merrill, Georgia Drew. *History of Coos County*. Somersworth, New Hampshire: New Hampshire Publishing Company, 1972 reprint of 1888 edition.

Murphy, Jr., Thomas W. *The Wedding Cake House: The World of George W. Bourne*. Kennebunk, Maine: Thomas Murphy, 1978.

Musgrove, Eugene, ed. *The White Hills in Poetry*. Boston and New York: Houghton Mifflin Company, 1912.

Olds, Elizabeth Fagg. *Women of the Four Winds*. Boston: Houghton Mifflin Company, 1985.

Pilley, Dorothy. *Climbing Days*. New York: Harcourt, Brace and Company, 1935.

Rowan, Peter and June Hammond Rowan, ed. *Mountain Summers*. Gorham, N.H.: Gulfside Press, 1995.

Slosson, Annie Trumbull. *Fishin' Jimmy*. New York: C. Scribner's Sons, 1898.

Slosson, Annie Trumbull. *Seven Dreamers*. New York: Harper & Brothers, 1891.

Slosson, Annie Trumbull. *White Christopher*. Philadelphia: Sunday School Times Co., 1905.

Somers, Rev. A.N. *History of Lancaster, New Hampshire*. Concord, New Hampshire: The Rumford Press, 1899.

Spaulding, John H. *Guide and Historical Relics of the White Mountains*. Mount Washington, New Hampshire: J.H. Spaulding, 1858.

Speare, Eva A., ed. *New Hampshire Folk Tales*. Littleton, N.H.: Courier Printing Co., 1964.

Tolles Jr., Bryant F., ed. *The Grand Resort Hotels and Tourism in the White Mountains*. Concord, N.H.: New Hampshire Historical Society, 1995.

Underhill, Miriam. *Give Me the Hills*. Riverside, Ct.: The Chatham Press, Inc., 1971.

Varney, Marion L. *Hart's Location in Crawford Notch*. Portsmouth, New Hampshire: Peter E. Randall Publisher, 1997.

Walden, Arthur Treadwell. *Leading a Dog's Life*. Boston and New York: Houghton Mifflin Co., 1931.

Waterman, Guy and Laura Waterman. *Forest and Crag: A History of Hiking, Trail Blazing, and Adventure in the Northeast Mountains.*. Boston: Appalachian Mountain Club, 1989.

Waterman, Guy and Laura Waterman. *Yankee Rock and Ice*. Harrisburg, Pa.:Stackpole Books, 1993.

Willey, Benjamin G. *Incidents in White Mountain History.* Boston: Nathaniel Noyes, 1855.

Williams, Cicely. *Women on the Rope: The Feminine Share in Mountain Adventure.* London: George Allen & Unwin, 1973.

ARTICLES

Ayres, Philip W. "Is New England's Wealth in Danger?" *New England Magazine,* four installments: March, April, May, June 1908.

Burt, Frank H. "The White Mountains Forty Years Ago." *Appalachia,* December 1916.

Boylan, James. "Annie Trumbull Slosson: A Local Colorist from Cannon Square." *Historical Footnotes* (Bulletin of the Stonington Historical Society), August 1985.

Cook, Edith. W. "A Reconnaissance on the Carter Range." *Appalachia,* April 1884.

Cross, George Newton. "Randolph Yesterdays." *Appalachia,* December 1916.

Fay, Charles. "Mount Passaconaway." *Appalachia,* January 1892.

Fobes, Charles B. "Metallak—Mollocket—Sabattus." *Appalachia,* December 1955.

Fowler-Billings, Katharine. "The Long Road to Save the Green Hills of Conway, New Hampshire." *Appalachia,* June 15, 1992.

Goodrich, N.L. "The Four-thousanders." *Appalachia,* December 1931.

Henderson, Ken. "In Memoriam: Elizabeth Knowlton." *Appalachia,* December 15, 1989.

Henderson, Ken. "In Memorian: Robert Underhill." *Appalachia,* Winter 1984-85.

Kilbourne, Frederick W. "Primus the Scribe." *Appalachia,* June 1931.

Leich, Jeffrey. "The Stone Hotels of Mount Washington." *Appalachia,* June 15, 1997.

MacGregor, Milton E. "The Best Friend a Hutman Ever Had." *Appalachia,* June 1963.

Pychowska, Mrs. L.D. and Pychowska, Miss Marian M. "Baldcap Mountain." *Appalachia,* July 1880.

Ricker, Charlotte. "The Wilderness: Wild Places and Rugged Peaks First Visited by Woman." *The White Mountain Echo,* August 16, 1882; September 2, 1882; September 9, 1882.

Scott, A.E. "The Twin Mountain Range." *Appalachia,* April 1883.

Slosson, Annie Trumbull. "Experiences of a Collector. " *Bulletin of the Brooklyn Entomological Society*. April 1917.

Stone, M. Isabella. "Mt. Waternomee and the Blue Ridge." *Appalachia*, December 1884.

Tuckerman, Frederick. "The Golden Age of the White Hills," *Appalachia*, February 1926.

Tuckerman, Frederick. "The White Mountains in the Early Seventies." *Appalachia*, April 1924.

Underhill, Miriam. "Elephant Tale." *Appalachia*, June 15, 1966.

Underhill, Miriam. "Manless Alpine Climbing." *National Geographic*, August 1934.

Wallner, Jeffrey S. "Butterflies and Trout: Annie Trumbull Slosson and W.C. Prime in Franconia." *Historical New Hampshire*, Fall 1977.

Whitman, Miss M.F. "A Climb through Tuckerman's Ravine." *Appalachia*, June 1877.

Acknowledgements

IN WRITING this book, I was fortunate that the Dartmouth College Library, which has perhaps the finest White Mountain collection in the world, is located within a half-hour drive of my home. Many thanks to the staff of the Rauner Special Collections Library for their assistance. I also want to thank the staffs at several other fine libraries: the Tuck Library of the New Hampshire Historical Society, the Mount Washington Observatory Library, the North Conway Library, and the Conway Library. And a special thanks to Sue Filkins of the Tracy Memorial Library in New London, New Hampshire, for arranging inter-library loans.

Relatives of some of the women in the book helped greatly by answering my questions and, in some cases, providing photographs. My sincerest thanks to Robert Underhill, Nicholas Helburn, Margaret Helburn Kocher, Elizabeth Gren, Pam Carlson, and George and Rachel Billings.

For assistance in locating and copying photographs, I am indebted to John Gerber of the AMC, David Smolen of the New Hampshire Historical Society, Peter Crane and Sean Doucette of the Mount Washington Observatory, Roland Goodbody of the University of New Hampshire, George and Sally Zink, Peter Rowan and June Hammond R   owan, Laura Waterman, Natalie Davis, Dwight Wilder, and Bob Shevett.

Maggie Stier kindly read the manuscript and offered many excellent suggestions. John Mudge provided guidance and invaluable editorial expertise as he thoroughly reviewed the manuscript for inconsistencies and stylistic errors. In addition, my son Jeff St.Onge, a journalist, read and made insightful comments on several chapters. The help of all three is deeply appreciated.

Finally, I wish to thank my husband Foster Boardman who joined me on research trips to the White Mountains and elsewhere and who was unfailingly patient and cheerful while I spent long hours writing. This book could not have been written without his support.

Index

Photo Credits

Unless noted below, all illustrations are courtesy of the Durand Press.

CHAPTER TWO
15: courtesy of the Appalachian Mountain Club. 22: courtesy of the Dartmouth College Library, Rauner Special Collections.

CHAPTER FOUR
33, 36, 38: courtesy of the Mount Washington Observatory.

CHAPTER FIVE
43: courtesy of the Beverly Historical Society. 46: from the *Journal of the New York Entomological Society*, December 1926. 48, 50: courtesy of the Mount Washington Observatory. 52: courtesy of the New Hampshire Historical Society.

CHAPTER SIX
57: courtesy of the Monastery of Saint Dominic, reprinted, by permission, from *Mountain Summers* edited by Peter Rowan and June Hammond Rowan. 64: courtesy of the Mount Washington Observatory. 67: courtesy of the Framingham Historical Society, reprinted, by permission, from *Mountain Summers* edited by Peter Rowan and June Hammond Rowan.

CHAPTER SEVEN
80, 82: courtesy of George and Sally Zink. 85: courtesy of the New Hampshire Historical Society.

CHAPTER EIGHT
91, 92, 96, 108: courtesy of the Appalachian Mountain Club. 94: courtesy of Margaret Helburn Kocher. 97: courtesy of the Milne Special Collections and Archives Department, University of New Hampshire Library, Durham, NH. 110: courtesy of Foster Boardman.

CHAPTER NINE
113: courtesy of the Mount Washington Observatory. 114: courtesy of the Appalachian Mountain Club.

CHAPTER TEN
122: courtesy of the Society of Woman Geographers. 126, 128: courtesy of Laura Waterman. 130: courtesy of the Dartmouth College Library, Rauner Special Collections.

CHAPTER ELEVEN
139, 140: courtesy of George and Rachel Billings.

About the Author

Julie Boardman is a professional writer whose work has appeared in *Appalachia*, the *Sierra Club Magazine*, *Connecticut Magazine*, *Connecticut Audubon*, *Ford Times*, and many other publications. Since moving to New London, New Hampshire, in 1990, she has hiked extensively throughout New England. She is a member of the Appalachian Mountain Club, the White Mountain Four Thousand Footer Club, and the New England Four Thousand Footer Club.